NUMEROLOGY

Your Love and Relationship Guide

Sonia Ducie, AIN

ELEMENT

Shaftesbury, Dorset ● Boston, Massachusetts ● Melbourne, Victoria

133.335

First published in the UK in 1999 by
Element Books Limited
Shaftesbury, Dorset SP7 8BP

Published in the USA in 1999 by
Element Books, Inc.
160 North Washington Street, Boston, MA 02114

Published in Australia in 1999 by
Element Books and distributed
by Penguin Australia Limited
487 Maroondah Highway, Ringwood, Victoria 3134

Cover design by Slatter-Anderson
Text illustrations by Frances Wilson
Design by Dale Tomlinson
Phototypeset by Intype London Ltd
Printed and bound in Great Britain by
Biddles Ltd, Guildford & King's Lynn

British Library Cataloguing in Publication data available
Library of Congress Cataloging in Publication data available

ISBN 1 86204 331 0

To Life

Contents

Part 1 · **Introduction**

Part 2 · **The Love Guide**

Part 3 · **Your Relationship Comparison Numbers**

PART 1

INTRODUCTION

1

About Numerology

NUMEROLOGY is the psychology, philosophy and science of numbers. It is a realistic and powerful tool because it creates within your mind the space to delve deep into your subconscious, and to reveal information previously unthought of or untold. Numbers contain infinite possibilities or potential as they are clear mirrors – like water – of the never ending evolution of mankind, as they mirror time itself. They also reveal information about your life and your relationships which can clarify and mirror back to you some simple truths.

All life is linked; the earth, the moon, the stars, other planets and solar systems are all contained within the whole. They influence you as much as you influence them with your thoughts, your actions and your intent, because you are part of life. It is incredible to think that what happens in another country across the world can influence you and your relationships, or a powerful strong magnetic moon can play a part too. For example, a volcanic eruption across the globe may mean no rain for long periods of time. This dry weather, particularly in summer when it is hot, can make you more irritable and stressed, which in turn influences all your relationships.

Numbers are holistic because they link together the past, the present and the future as part of the whole. Numbers are, in effect, ways by which you learn and grow, and growth is organic and definite and results from the changes which you experience in your life. Science, biology, geometry and art, medicine, economics and mathematics – numbers are the foundations of existence. They are the roots of evolution, and the key to joy as they bring with them awareness as you go about your daily life.

In numerology all numbers divide down to between 1 and 9, and each number is what is called a cycle or a trend. If you take any number, like 2,764 for example, and add it up, which in this case adds to a 19, then 10, then a 1, it gives you a final digit between 1 and 9. All life evolves in cycles of 1 to 9, because these are the simplest denominations of all life. In fact, life and its lessons are simple, and refining life to its simplicity is what helps to reveal the truths of life, the Holy Grail. Life revolves around cycles, and the cycles within cycles. There are large cycles like that of life, death and rebirth, and smaller cycles, day and night, the four seasons (dependent upon which part of the world you live in), weekly cycles, and of course moon cycles, and so on. These can all be observed by applying numerology to help you understand their significance and the role they play in your life. Numerology helps you understand more about your inner universe which is of course mirrored out in the external world around you.

Numerology is also a key to developing your intuition, and it can help you with your personal development too. When numerology is applied to the numbers in your date of birth and to your names (each letter of the alphabet translates into a number between 1 and 26), these

4

numbers or energies spring to life. They reveal information about your psychological patterns of behaviour, your personality, your life purpose or direction, goals, karmic responsibilities, and the annual temporary cycles (called your personal year cycles) which influence each year of your life. All these numbers can be drawn up into a numerological chart, which is unique to each person. The numbers in the various areas of your chart influence every aspect of your life, including your relationships. Therefore, if you are aware of the power of these numbers as they influence your life, you will be in a better position to make the most of all your relationships.

In Chapter 4 you can find out exactly how to work out your numerology chart, which will give you the tools to discover your strengths, challenges and potential within all of your relationships. Every number in your chart is important but your Personality and Life Purpose Numbers carry the strongest influence. Sometimes your Personality wants one thing and the influence from your Life Purpose Numbers mean you need something else. These two numbers can indeed mean you feel like two different people at times, both parts of yourself trying to work out what's best, and doing the best you can, while rubbing up against the other.

Each number between 1 and 9 contains positive and negative or challenging influences as part of its potential. Zero contains the ideas and concepts from which all numbers are born, and therefore contains the potential for all life. Numbers also contain physical, emotional, mental and spiritual elements in them, and relate to the elements of earth, fire, air and water too. Numbers can be active (masculine) or yang (1, 3, 5, 7, 9) or passive (feminine) or yin (2, 4, 6, 8); Yin and Yang are the masculine and feminine polarities within all life and which help to form a balance.

You also recognize the term 'left or right brained' in relation to how you carry out your life; left brained for masculine logical characteristics, or right brained for feminine creative characteristics. But everyone uses both left and right to some degree. However, you may have more masculine or more feminine aspects influencing you, which can be seen from the numbers in your chart. Of course, sometimes you use more of one or the other at different times during your life, and even different times during the day.

Sometimes two people can have the same date of birth but seem like completely different people. This is because they portray more of the feminine or more of the masculine qualities of the numbers in their chart either in a more positive or challenging way, and at different times. Of course, even two people who are very similar like twins have different names, and this can make an enormous difference to their potential life experiences, so that they share the same birth date but explore their numbers in their own unique way.

With numerology you are not your numbers because that would be like saying a number is a solid brick and it's not: numbers are empty vessels full of potential. Numbers simply influence your life, but you have free will and it is up to you how you best utilize these intricate energies. For example, if you were born on the 6th of the month (6 Personality) it means you may be caring (a strength) or uncaring (a challenge) at different times – you choose!

However, you are neither totally good nor bad, and

every human being has the same potential to choose connection or separation, love or fear, expansion or
contraction – it's as simple as that. Everyone has a shadow
side: qualities about yourself you may like to keep hidden
because you think they are 'bad' – your faults. Your
shadow side is very important because it contains aspects
of yourself which need to be brought into the 'light' and
healed. Numerology highlights the shadow side from the
numbers in your chart, so that your fears of the bits of
yourself which you try to disown can be understood. It can
help you to love and accept yourself, to be yourself, and to
recognize that everyone is learning similar lessons in life
(based on the numbers 1 to 9). Working on your faults
means that life doesn't get too dull and boring, which
would happen if there was were no challenges in life,
particularly within your relationships!

Numbers, like energy, flow, and each number flows into
the next, which is how nature works too; each lifetime
flows into the next, and where you go and what you need
is based on the lessons you have learned before. Your life
now influences the whole of your future, and making the
most out of your life right now by taking responsibility for
yourself can help you to paint a brighter future.

HISTORY

All cultures from around the world have used – and continue to use – one form of numerology or another,
although they may call their methods by different names;
Divination, Geometria, Esoteric Numerology, Pythagorian
Numerology, and so on. The methods vary but the

understanding is the same; numbers give you information about life.

It is believed that the ancient Hindus, Chinese, Tibetans and Egyptians used numerology a great deal as it played a large part in their cultures. Pythagoras the Greek mathematician was also a numerologist around 600 BC. He figures greatly in modern-day numerology because of the popularity of his Pythagorian method based on the numbers 1 to 9.

NUMBERS EVOLVE

Of course, numbers can be counted infinitely. In addition to the system 1 to 9, today numerologists also recognize 'master numbers' which are the numbers 11, 22, 33 and so on up to 99. Master numbers are numbers which can influence you by making you aware of the gifts you can use to help others 'in service' with the intensity of the qualities they contain. For example, a 55 in your chart means you may have a real gift for speech, languages or communication and you may use these in some way to help others. These numbers are doubled because they are requiring you to learn their lessons quickly – like life bringing its qualities to your awareness in a big way. However the numbers 1 to 9 are the most powerful because they contain condensed energies which influence your life. Some numerologists even work on the system of numbers 1 to 81 ($9 \times 9 = 81$) because it is the largest denomination of the number 9, but they still lay emphasis on the final digit of 1 to 9 as being of most importance.

You are surrounded by numbers and numbers are

making history today by revealing the experiences they contain. Enjoy your date with this book and let it reveal to you some better known secrets of life and relationships.

2

Numerology and Relationships

WHAT are relationships? What immediately springs to mind are your interactions between yourself and your friends, workmates, your lover or partner, and so on. But actually relationships go much further than that because you are also in relationship to everything within your environment, which includes yourself!

Your first relationship began after you were conceived when you first started to relate to your mother in the womb, and externally to your father. Even in the womb you were aware of your mother's external surroundings and the outside world. You were probably subconsciously aware of the dynamics of your parents' relationship as well. Perhaps you were born into a caring and loving home, or fortunate enough to be born in peace-time in the 'free' West, or blessed with material security . . . or enough to survive – lucky you. Perhaps you were born in a cold, warm or hot climate so you have a relationship with that particular kind of weather too. Even the place where you were born – a village, a city, the country – you have a relationship with, and its beliefs, structures and culture strongly influence you.

During the first seven years (in Numerology 7 represents

completion) everything in your environment and everyone whom you were in relationship with played a large part in your life. This is because it is your conditioning in childhood which forms the basis of your psychological patterns of behaviour which influence the rest of your life – 'the formative years' as they are called. Numerology brings awareness to these patterns so that you can clearly see your strengths and your challenges, for example, ways in which you block yourself in your relationships with others. It can therefore help you to release childhood memories or traumas that may have been locked away, and help you to fulfil your potential.

You are connected to the world in which you live, but your immediate relationships with your friends, family, lovers, workmates and animals form a large part of your conscious awareness within your daily life. Everyone shares the same basic needs for love and sex, food, shelter, warmth, and work, but the patterns you weave within your relationships are intricate and wonderful and are inspiring. Your relationships teach you more about yourself and about life. They encourage you to learn to give and take and to share yourself with those around you. Love makes the world go around, with its many forms and disguises, and in its simplicity supports and nurtures your growth. Love is inclusive and is available to everyone and everything. Love is in the air because it sustains you, and you are in relationship with that every human moment of your life.

Your environment is constantly changing, and so are your relationships – change is one thing you can be one hundred per cent certain of on this planet. Even your cells are constantly changing and rearranging . . . life is always

11

on the move. Therefore adapting to your constantly changing environment as expressed through your relationships can help you make the most out of your life. Numerology can reveal more about who you are, and in what ways you are relating to those around you within the uncertainty of these relationships. In one way, if you were certain that your lover would always be there when you wanted him or her or that your husband would always be faithful, it may seem ideal. But uncertainty can also add a spice of excitement because you never know just what is around the corner, and because it can drive you to put more effort into your relationships or be more grateful for what you have right now. Trust is one of the most important aspects within your relationships.

COMPETITION

From the moment you were born you have been competing with one thing or another; for love, food, attention, appraisal, acceptance, bigger and better . . . more, more and more. Perhaps you were brighter than your sister or brother, learned quickly, were top of the class, ran the fastest, and so on. Some religions believe that you are the lucky one to be born on planet earth because only one seventh of souls incarnate – or are conceived. Indeed, even sperm compete to reach and fertilize the egg which created you. Can you imagine what synchronicity it must have taken to get you here . . . the competition was enormous!

So make the most out of your time here . . . live in the moment, enjoy every minute, live your life fully, love and learn. New opportunities are available to everyone but it is up to you to take them and make them work.

This inbuilt but subconscious memory of competition also carries into all your relationships. For example, you want to earn more money than your boyfriend (with 8 in your chart) to feel more powerful than him. Or you may buy all the trendiest clothes (you may have a 6 in your chart) to make yourself more attractive so that your lover's eye doesn't wander. Perhaps you compulsively go to the gym (number 1) so that you keep your body in perfect shape, even though you don't enjoy it, to compete with your best friend, and so on. 'But I'm not competitive in the least' some of you may exclaim. But if you are honest with yourself and you look closely, you will usually find at least one occasion when you did compete, even if it was in the most subtle way. Knowing everyone competes can in one way take the pressure off you, to accept that this is a part of everyday life. Of all the numbers or cycles 1 to 9, number 8 brings in some of the strongest forms of competition and if you have this number in your chart you may be fully aware of its presence.

Of course in adult years you learn to discriminate about whether to compete or not consciously, and you may choose to view competition in a different way. That is, you and I may be competing but we can join together and work together for the same result. For example, we may both want to be the local politician because we both have the same goal in mind of improving conditions for the community, but we both have different ways or ideas about how this can be done. So in competition to win the electoralship for the position we can be aware that the other person has some good ideas like you, and that no matter who gets elected, either of you can help towards the good of the community.

Competition can sometimes be good for you because it keeps you on your toes. For example, if two people are competing to win a race then they not only inspire the other to run faster, but also the other players make more of an effort too. However, using competition as a tool of retaliation and anger doesn't benefit anyone because it wipes you out (fighting is exhausting) and it usually creates an equally disturbing response which you may not have bargained for. Competition can therefore spur you on to do better when you understand the goal, and can then be used in a wonderfully constructive way to bring positive results.

Indeed, even in this world of competition you may be aware that the most fundamental and necessary quality to get you through life is that of co-operation. Even though you may be competitive without co-operation at some level with others, you may not achieve harmonious relationships. For example, if there was no co-operation between you and your lover you may not agree on a time for a date, where to lay your hat, and so on. If you have a passion for watching movies and he likes to socialize and go out and about you'd see each other less if there was no compromise or co-operation. Number 2 in the cycle of 1 to 9 mirrors the energy of co-operation very strongly, and if you have this number in your chart then you are particularly learning about this quality or strength.

BE YOURSELF

Even if you do not consciously compete with others that element is always there. However, the best you can ever do is to simply be yourself: not trying to be or do something because someone or society decides it's OK or that you are credit worthy, not trying to dress in a certain way to conform to what your partner or friends want . . . be yourself! This means following your own truth, making your own mistakes, taking responsibility for yourself, living, learning and moving on.

The way you learn about yourself is by being in relation-ship to life – situations – and to others, and playing your part in life. With everyone you meet or whom you talk to you are sharing the learning experience of relationships, and you are helping each other to learn and develop. Of course, you have choice, and you may need to learn the same lessons over and over again until you have understood them – this is life. For example, if your boss has told you that he will not tolerate your moods and temperamental behaviour every Monday morning and kindly asks you to be aware of this and you ignore his warnings, then you may eventually find yourself without a job. By being you, your environment teaches you what you need to learn. You learn by experience, and by experiencing who you are fully, you can become more you, and it brings you deeper into life.

When you feel comfortable and safe within yourself you become very magnetic and sexy, and you shine because you have integrity or you are at one with yourself. People sense this and find you very attractive – it inspires them to be themselves, and allows them to feel comfortable too.

All famous people in the fields of the sciences, medicine, literature, music, art, religion and politics, and inventors of all kinds, are successful because they have learned to be themselves, for example, Gandhi (politician), Mother Teresa and Princess Diana (humanitarian), and currently Bill Gates (industry), Stephen Spielberg (the arts), Richard Branson (entrepreneur), and singers like Boy George and Elton John (for their individuality and music). The list is endless. These people are no doubt aware of their faults and also their challenges, but they have made the most of their potential. These people are mirrors of society and are teaching you more about the world in which you live. Numerology mirrors your potential and so brings awareness and reveals ways in which you can explore more of the real you, so that you can become happier within yourself, within the world, and within all your relationships.

MIRRORS

Know thyself, heal thyself, and you heal others too. By healing yourself you are helping to heal others because everyone is but a part of the whole. All relationships are healing and constructive on one level or another. Your relationships are helping to heal the parts of you which need bringing into wholeness, so that you can fulfil your potential and become the most you can be. Have you ever said, 'I feel stronger from that relationship and although I was sad . . . it was traumatic at the time . . . it has helped me grow'? But what determines the situations you need to experience for your growth in the first place? It's all in your numbers. By observing the numbers in your date of birth and your names, you can become more aware of the types of experiences you are more likely to attract.

Like attracts like, so if you have a 3 in your chart – which means you may love roaming around and your freedom – you may attract someone to you who is dealing with issues around freedom too. For example, they may try to tie you down in a relationship, or perhaps you try to tie them down so that they pull away or want more freedom in their relationship with you. This is highlighted particularly when you or they have a 3 or a 5 in your chart. Numbers are moving particles of energy, and you may find you keep attracting people with the same energy or certain numbers to you (because they are in your chart, or missing from your chart so you look for them in others). This is in order to mirror back to you the lessons which you need to learn, and to reflect back to them qualities which they need to learn about too.

Mirroring also happens instantaneously with the situations you find yourself in with your relationship to life. For example, when you are in a happy-go-lucky mood and you are singing with the birds at sunrise have you noticed that your day goes well and you attract really positive people – even if you don't you remain blissfully happy anyway? On other days, when you are thinking negatively or in a bad mood, everything gets on top of you or it just becomes 'one of those days'. This mirroring and karma (you get back what you give out) means that the more you portray positive aspects of the numbers in your chart, the more positive results you will find within all your relationships.

Sometimes you give to one person and find you don't

receive the same back. But you may find someone else gives a lot to you and you do not appear to give them the same back. So in the end your relationships balance out. However, when you give, you naturally receive on some level anyway. From your thoughts and beliefs, your mind-sets and your actions you create your future right now. So in that way you are contributing every moment towards the situations you find yourself experiencing in life.

Everyone and everything around you is in your life for a reason, because it is mirroring something back to you which you need to know and understand, and learn from. Children are wonderful mirrors because they are so open and natural and say what they feel and think with very little discrimination. Children take some numbers from their mother's and their father's charts, which set up areas of compatibility and clashes between parents and children. This happens particularly during the teenage years when they are learning to individualize and to be more them-selves. If you are a parent you can see parts of yourself mirrored back to you in front of your very eyes; qualities from your numerology chart, and from your life which you are learning to accept, love and transform.

Within all your relationships there are natural cycles of expansion and contraction – times when they run smoothly, and challenging times which may seem to go on for ever and which you need to work through. You are in relationship with others so that you can teach each other about yourselves from the mirroring that goes on. People come together and drift apart when the mirroring is recognized and when what you can learn from each other is complete. That is, you see yourself in the mirror, perhaps stay around to polish that mirror so that you really understand some specific quality or lesson, and then move on. This explains why in some relationships people suddenly split up, or why others recognize where they are and choose to move on amicably or not, or why some people drift apart slowly over many years in which case they are still learning from each other.

Sometimes a person will be in your life for only days or weeks, or you may spend your lifetime in relationship with them which means you are mirroring and learning many things. When one person features very strongly in your life sometimes it is because you have a 'karmic' relationship, meaning you have many ties with them from the past (lives). This is often the case when you meet someone and you think, 'I know them already.' You may also think you know or understand someone and know what they are about because they share such similar qualities and attributes as you, and you recognize these.

In life you can learn the same lessons from many different people. For example if you are learning to be independent (one of the qualities of the number 1), your parents, your friends, your lover, your work colleagues, and so on, may all be teaching you about the same lesson. They may be teaching you about independence by encouraging you to do things on your own, or in other ways. Perhaps you bring up a child on your own so your child is teaching you about independence too.

ON WHICH LEVELS DO YOU RELATE?

Numerology helps you to know and understand yourself and to find out about which levels – physically, emotionally, mentally or spiritually – you are mirroring and relating to people around you. For example, if you have a spiritual number in your chart – 7 for instance – you still work and live in the physical world but it means that you have many lessons to learn about spirituality. Look at your chart and compare it to the numbers below.

PHYSICAL: 4 5
relates to things on the physical level
EMOTIONAL: 2 3 6
relates emotionally, very sensitive
MENTAL: 1 8
relates to the intellect, mind
SPIRITUAL: 7 9
relates to spiritual connection within self and others

If you have more of one or another of one particular number in your numerology chart – they are recurrent – or if numbers are missing from your chart, then these levels and qualities need to be developed or used and applied strongly.

To understand this a little further let's look and see on what levels John and Laura are relating to people in their lives, based on the numbers from their date of birth and their names. John lives in Sydney. He is married to Laura. John relates to Laura physically and they enjoy living together and sex too. They relate emotionally by supporting each other, and spiritually they share a deep connection with each other. However, they do not relate mentally. John relates mentally to his best friend Peter because they studied the same subjects together at university and they enjoy discussing their interests.

Laura relates to her mother Mary mentally (they think the same), and emotionally (they share their problems), but she relates very strongly spiritually to her father Simon (they are totally connected and share the same spiritual outlook about life).

It is rare for you to relate to one person on every different level, or to satisfy every level. Even if you do, it may be only for a very short time, which is why you need different people in your life. It is clear to see that everyone mirrors many different qualities to each other, but the lessons are simple based on the numbers 1 to 9 in your chart and you can learn all about them in this book.

TIMING

Timing is everything in life – or rather everything has its own time, and this includes your relationships. Timing is as relevant on the first occasion when you are trying to get together with someone as it is when you have been in relationship with them for a long time. However, no matter how much you plan, 'Yes, I'd like to see you at 6 o'clock next Friday,' other elements – the unexpected ones – may step in. The train was delayed, you had to go to the dentist or to a meeting suddenly, you got flu . . . and so on. Time asks you to learn to be flexible, and to trust that even if you didn't meet your date that night, if you're meant to, you will meet later on. The best plans of mice and men go astray, which is as a result of the unexpected. It has been said that eighty per cent of the universe is unexplored and unknown, which means there is a twenty per cent probability and eighty per cent chance of relationships going the way you want them to! In all your relationships this makes enjoying the moment essential and being together appear a luxury!

You may be in an idyllic romantic relationship with the best partner in the world, right now, or you may be full of bloom after giving birth to your first child, or feel wonderful for winning the confidence and support of your boss. This is happening now, but time is ticking by, nothing stays the same and perfect situations can change for ever. Making the most of your relationships by learning about yourself from the numbers in your chart can help you to make the most out of them right now.

Sometimes in life you may seem to take two steps forward and one step back. But you never return to where you were originally – you move on having learned by experience from what the people in your life were teaching and mirroring back to you, and learning to be yourself. Timing calls for patience, and to trust that where you are right now in your relationships is where you are meant to be. If you are saying, 'Hurry up, I want to get promoted,' to your boss, 'Hurry up, let's get married,' to your fiancee, or demanding things from those around you, then realize that if you try to push situations they rarely work out the way you want because you are trying to go against nature or time. You may however get what you need, although this may vary from what you want.

Take a look at Melissa (whose name adds up to a 6) and James (adds up to a 3). Melissa and James met each other at college. They went out together a few times but Melissa wasn't ready for a sexual relationship and James paid more attention to wanting sex with her than friendship, so they quickly drifted apart. Melissa was in her first year of college and, liking her independence, she wasn't too upset by not having a boyfriend because she was enjoying herself and exploring her individuality (number 1). James was in

22

his third year of college and wanting a bit of fun (number 3), and sex. Melissa and James married separately, but fifteen years later synchronicity brought them together again. Now divorced, they rekindled their relationship on different levels – emotionally and sexually – beyond how they related together before, realized what they had missed, and soon happily got married. They 'clicked'. Both types of relationship they have experienced together were right at the time.

It may work out differently, of course. For example, have you ever found yourself in an intimate relationship and then bumped into that person years later and thought, 'Whatever did I see in that person, they're not even attractive, how could I have had sex with them, or even married them?' Well, what you saw in them has not changed but the qualities they were mirroring in you have been recognized and integrated so that they lose their attraction. Of course, you may choose to get together on another level, perhaps a platonic relationship if it was sexual before, or a sexual relationship if it was platonic. Or it may be you work together instead of being lovers, and so on.

As you see, timing is everything, and from your numerology chart and your Personal Year Number (this number changes every year of your life), you can see when you are more likely to get restless, up and leave, want commitment, and so on.

CYCLES

When you first meet your partner you are in the first day of the first week of the first month and year of your relationships, and 1 influences new beginnings and new opportunities. This applies whatever kind of relationship you are in; intimate or otherwise. It is interesting to note how long somebody stays around in your life as you trace the influences of each day, week or year you spend together in relationship. Being aware of these numerology cycles can help you to make the most out of your time together.

Ever heard of the 'seven-year itch?' In nature 7 likes to bear fruit, but a tree can only bear fruit if the roots were planted firmly in the ground, had regular water, received warmth from the sun, and was looked after and nurtured with due care and consideration. Relationships are like that, and in numerology the 7 means the tree either bears fruit or it fails to bring a harvest. On the seventh day, week, year of your relationship therefore it is a time for completion and what happens will be as a direct result of the energy you have put into those previous six days, weeks or years.

The eighth cycle is for taking stock from your previous seven cycles and revaluating, the ninth cycle is for readjusting and thinking through what you need to take with you into your next nine-year cycle within your relationships.

MELTDOWN

No matter who you are, what you do, or what decisions you take in life (you make the best choices you can at the time), you are always contributing to the world because you are in one way or another relating to the world through your relationships, and allowing others to learn by relating to you. You are neither good nor bad, but like everyone else are learning the lessons you need (based on the numbers in your chart) from the experiences you have on this rich planet earth.

3

Making the Most of
the Love Guide

This book can be your companion as you travel on your journey throughout your life. Numbers are everywhere, and even a simple understanding of some of the qualities and potential contained within each number or cycle of 1 to 9 can help you on your path. The information in this book can open up your eyes to a new way of looking at yourself and all your relationships. It can do this simply by encouraging you to view everyone – from your local shopkeeper to your friends, family, partner and work associates – as wonderful mirrors who are teaching you more about yourself and about life.

BEGIN AT THE BEGINNING

Numbers are energies which influence you, but you are not your numbers. Each number flows into the next and therefore you can have many numbers influencing you. For example, if you were born on the 17th of the month (17 adds up to an 8), then you may be influenced by some of the qualities of the 16 (= 7) or/and the 18 (= 9), the days before and after you were born. However, the day on

26

which you were born has the strongest influence. If you have a double digit in your chart, then you may like to look up all the numbers individually which are influencing you. For example, taking the example above, if you were born on the 17th of the month then the single digit it adds up to between 1 and 9 has the strongest influence. So for the 17 it is an 8. You can also read about the numbers 1 and 7 (17) because they will influence you too.

When reading about the numbers in your chart, you may recognize some but not all of the qualities within yourself. This is because each number offers some *potential* attributes, and you may not need to experience all these aspects in this lifetime.

When you first start working with numerology it may take a while before you can get 'a feel' for the overall picture, because there are many different numbers in your chart. But after a while you start to see the picture, and the more you practise numerology the easier it is to stop thinking too hard about the process and simply allow it to happen.

STEP 1

In order for you to work out your chart you need to read Chapter 4: Working Out Your Numerology Chart. Here it will show you how to work out your Personality and Life Path Numbers from your date of birth, and your Karma or Wisdom Number from your Names, and also your Goal Number from your Christian or first name. It will also show you how to work out your yearly influence number or Personal Year Number (which changes from birthday to birthday).

STEP 2

In Chapter 5, The Love Guide, you can read about the numbers 1 to 9 and about your relationships with yourself, your friends, lovers, family, and work colleagues, and about qualities influencing your sex life too. This chapter highlights your potential, your strengths and your challenges.

STEP 3

Next, read Chapter 6, Working Out Comparison Numbers, which shows you how to compare different aspects of your chart with others.

STEP 4

In Chapter 7, Comparing Your Charts, you can read about some of the lessons you and your friends, lover, partner, family, workmates (indeed anyone in your life) are learning about within your relationship together.

STEP 5

Finally, Chapter 8 gives you three true case histories (with fictitious names) for you to refer to as guidelines.

FINALLY

Numbers encourage you to delve deep into your subconscious and even when you have read about the qualities of the numbers your intuition and your mind play a large part in revealing their little jewels. This is because the amount of qualities one number contains is endless and no book would be big enough to accommodate them all . . . Relax, have fun learning, and enjoy your journey.

4

Working Out Your Numerology Chart

WORKING out your chart is simple, like anything, once you know how. Remember, each number in your chart influences your life, but the single digit – between 1 and 9 – is always the strongest.

YOUR DATE OF BIRTH AND YOUR NAMES

From your date of birth you can work out your Personality Number and your Life Purpose/Life Path Number, and your Personal Year Number. And from your names on your birth certificate you can work out your Karma or Wisdom Number, and your major Goal Number. All the numbers in your chart are important and they all interact with each other, but your Personality and Life Path Numbers play the most significant part in your life. These numbers act as catalysts for each other, helping you to realize your potential. They also highlight some of your key lessons in life. The way that these numbers react together in your chart is influenced by your Karma Number and your Major Goal Number, and even by your Personal Year Number.

YOUR PERSONALITY NUMBER

This number is taken from the day in the month on which you were born. For example, if you were born on the 4th, the number influencing your personality is a 4. If you were born on any number with two digits, that is on the 10th to the 31st of the month, then you add them up to form one single digit between 1 and 9. For example, the 25th = 7, so 7 influences your Personality. However, the 2 and the 5 have secondary influences and are important too, so take these into account by learning about these numbers too. Your Personality Number gives you your strengths, challenges and potential with regard to your psychological patterns of behaviour. This number is attributed to what you want in life for yourself.

YOUR LIFE PURPOSE / LIFE PATH NUMBER

To find out your Life Purpose Number you simply add up your whole date of birth, remembering to keep your day and month when you were born in its original form. For example, if you were born on 31.12.1978, then add up 31 and 12 (which equals 43), to the year in which you were born. Here 1978 adds up to 25. So add 43 and 25 which equals 68, and add this up to form a single digit which becomes 14 and then, added together, 5. So 5 is your Life Purpose Number with influences of the 68 and 14. Then you may like to read about the 6, 8, 1 and 4 to see these influences over your life too, but the 5 is always the strongest. This Life Purpose Number gives you your strengths, challenges and potential in relation to how you can 'work' with others in your life, and it relates to you doing 'what is needed' rather than what only you want or need. It reflects some of your Soul qualities and has a deeper meaning or influence over your life.

YOUR PERSONAL YEAR

To find out what number is influencing your current year (from birthday to birthday) simply follow the example. You take your day and month of birth, say the 3rd of January, and add them up, so 3 + 1 = 4. Then add up the year of your last birthday; if your last birthday was in 1999 this adds up to 28, 10, then a 1. To get your Personal Year vibration for your birthday 3rd January 1999 to 3rd January 2000, simply add 4 (day and month) to 1 (the year of your last birthday) which equals 5. So 5 is your current Personal Year vibration. This number influences you with its qualities, strengths, challenges and potential for one particular year. If your Personal Year Number is in your chart already (particularly as a Personality or Life Path Number) then this may make the experiences you are learning about more intense in a positive or challenging way according to how you respond. For example, if 5 is your Life Path Number and you are influenced by a 5 as your Personal Year vibration, then one of its qualities – change – may mean that this is intensified during that year: you may go through great changes. These changes may be physical, emotional, mental or spiritual, and in any or every area of your life.

The following issues are highlighted during each current personal year:

Year 1   new direction, opportunity
Year 2   decision-making, balance
Year 3   moving forwards and expanding
Year 4   security, survival
Year 5   general changes
Year 6   relationships
Year 7   completion
Year 8   karma, finding your strength
Year 9   letting go and letting in

However, because you function as part of the whole of humanity the Universal Year, the year you live in, also plays a large part in the experiences you may have. For example, 1999 adds up to $28 = 10 = 1$, so universally there is an influence of new direction this year.

YOUR KARMA OR WISDOM NUMBER

This number is taken by translating all the letters from the full name on your birth certificate into numbers, and then adding them up to find a single digit. First of all write down your name and translate it from the A to Z chart below.

1	A	J	S
2	B	K	T
3	C	L	U
4	D	M	V
5	E	N	W
6	F	O	X
7	G	P	Y
8	H	Q	Z
9	I	R	

Example:	Sarah	Jane	Delanie
	11918	1155	4531595 = 64/10 = 1
	= 20/2	= 12/3	= 32/5

In the example above, Sarah Jane's Karma or Wisdom Number is a 1. This number gives you indications of your karma from this lifetime or from past lives. It also gives you strengths, challenges and potential (which, if you have used these qualities in previous lives may be very strong). For example with 1 as a Karma Number Sarah Jane may have been a very knowledgeable person in the past, and uses this strength to help others. Sometimes she may use her accumulated wisdom to hurt others which is therefore a challenge which she is working to transform in this lifetime.

When we are born our parents are usually the ones who subconsciously choose the names for us which will help us with our lives, so that we each have the best potential to learn the lessons and to fulfil those goals we need to in this lifetime. However, if you wish to work out your Karma Number and you were adopted, or you do not have a birth certificate, then you can apply numerology to all the names by which you were first known. For example, perhaps you were called Mary Jane Smith by your guardians, in which case you apply numerology to those names.

Your birth names carry the strongest numerological influence over your whole life, and therefore over your relationships. Even if you get married and change your name then, or change it for any other reason, the influence from your birth names stays the same. However, a new married name brings qualities and aspects which are often somehow present in the chart already, to emphasize the qualities that the newly wed person needs to learn. If your name has been changed by marriage, you can bring those qualities influenced by your names and your whole numerological chart into your married life.

YOUR MAJOR GOAL

This is taken from your first name, Sarah (from the example above) which adds up to a 21 or a 3. This means that one of Sarah's goals is to learn to express herself, and she has her whole lifetime to work on this. The 2 and the 1 from the 21 also influence her goal, but the 3 has the strongest influence here. Your first name is important because everyone calls you by it – it is your personal imprint – and therefore its vibration has an enormous influence over your life.

Nicknames also influence you, but in the way that the person calling you by a nickname is projecting onto you some of the qualities that they think they see – or that they may like to see – in you. In addition, if you make up your own abbreviated name then you are strongly identifying with particular aspects of yourself when you go by it. For example, Susan may like to be called Susan at work, Sue at home or Suzie by her boyfriend to reflect how she identifies with specific people or adapts to different situations in her life. However, the influence of her whole first name, Susan, is always present.

THE QUICKIE

If you are going out on a date with a new boyfriend or girlfriend or you meet someone who you are going to have dealings with, or you are fascinated to find out more about how people work, look at their 'Quickie Number'. To find this simply add the first letter of your first and your surname or family name together. For example, Jenny Wright = J+W = 1+5 which equals 6. If your name has a prefix, like O'Donnell or McCartney, then add the first letter of the prefixes to the equation. For example, Jane O'Donnell = J+O+D = 11 = 2. This number highlights what you are projecting out to the world, and some qualities which you are learning about in this lifetime. So Jenny Wright (1+5) is a 6, and you can read about Number 6 in Part 2: The Love Guide. For example, she may have an appreciation for beauty, be loving and generous, and like fashion, music and good food, or she may be an idealist and a perfectionist too.

NUMEROLOGY

Remember that you can add up or subtract numbers any way you like because there is not just one method which is right and another wrong. For example, you may wish to add up all the vowels in your name, and then all your consonants, to see which other influences you have there. You can add up each of the individual names in your chart so that you can find out more about those too. You can get a feel for the rhythm of each name and add up what number you think each one vibrates to. For example, Sophi-a has a rhythm of 3, or John has a rhythm of 1. From your date of birth perhaps add up the month you were born in, or the year, separately to see how these numbers are influencing your life. Numbers speak to you, and by working with numerology you can develop your own way

of understanding more about your relationships with the
world in which you live. Once you have worked out your
numbers you can go on to read the relevant sections in
Part 2, in which you will be able to recognize and learn
about the qualities within relationships based upon the
numbers from all the different aspects of your chart.
Enjoy.

PART TWO

THE
LOVE
GUIDE

5

Lovers 1 to 9

LOVERS

ZERO is the number containing all potential, but in life number 1 is the beginning and the end of the universe because in life everything always goes back to the 1 or to the beginning. So if you comprehend what is being said here you can see that if you have a number 1 influencing your love life you are likely to think you're 'Number 1' or that you are the centre of the whole universe. This may mean you like life to revolve around you and while you can be a human dynamo (in all senses of the word) you can also be extremely self-centred. Imagine life without the number 1; imagine life without you in it (what a disaster for mankind that would be!). With a 1 you may be aloof, tucked away in your own world feeling very special and superior, with your lovers lying in wait as they try to catch your eye for some of your precious time and your precious energy. Whoever manages to penetrate your detached persona may well be the person to win your heart, or with whom you can find a purpose in life.

You can be very caring and giving and you have a willingness to go for what you want in life; you see the man or woman of your dreams and nothing will stop you. 'No' doesn't exist with many who are influenced by this number. And if your potential mate shows any resistance to you then you are challenged to break down their barriers until they surrender to your charms. You may even be forceful and make enemies as you force your way into relationships and into your lover's life. Perhaps you genuinely don't notice how many people are knocked down by your determination to fulfil your goals. Or you may be so self-centred that you don't notice anyone else in the equation or perhaps you simply don't care. Of course, with a 1, at times you may be too withdrawn and shy and even resist going for what you want, but in the course of events with a 1 these times are generally few and far between.

Sometimes when you see your perfect lover glittering before your very eyes you will scour your brain to try to work out exactly how you are going to get from A to B (which in your mind may mean getting your potential lover to go out on a date or into bed, or even just to speak to you!). The pioneering element within you springs to life. Or you may wonder how you are going to get from A to B even when you are involved in a sexual and intimate relationship with a scintillating lover. Sometimes your lack of self-esteem may mean that, for example at a party, you will spend a long time deliberating and working up your courage in order to approach your potential date. Perhaps to the extent that by the time you have thought up the perfect solution the chance passes you by as he or she slips into the arms of another suitor or disappears into the night. At other times you may be sat in the corner as you withdraw further into yourself just waiting for that special person to approach you.

However, with the energy and vitality of the number 1 influencing your life you are able to conjure up many lovers as you go on your journey. They are attracted to your strength and stamina and when you focus all that dynamic energy their way they can't help but fall by the wayside (or into your arms) and be duly flattered. You love to be flattered too, and like your lover to tell you how passionately and wonderfully you made love to them last night, or how intelligent you are. Yes, brains are important with a 1, and a mental workout can at times be more welcome and more stimulating than a physical one! Pillow talk takes on a whole new meaning here, a different dimension. And instead of whispering 'sweet nothings' you may recite to your lover the memoirs of political leaders, or expect your keen lover to recite to you 'a book at bedtime' before you sink into stimulated slumber, or disappear together beneath the sheets.

You like to feel unique, and the way to win your heart (or your head) is for your lover to constantly give you credit (even for breathing!) and to let you know that you are always his or her special one. Even better to put you on a pedestal or idolize you, sometimes to the extent that you become such a rare species that you simply do not need anyone else (or so you think), as you withdraw further into your splendid and glamourized isolation. A rare beauty or an icon in their field may be what you are seeking too; the untouchable lover with whom you can keep your independence and your cool detachment, and not have to reveal too much about the real you. Such a person may be very attractive to you, particularly if they are not interested in your most intimate feelings because they are aloof and set up high on their pedestal.

One of the lessons the number 1 is teaching you is to allow yourself to get deeply involved within your relationships — to learn to attach yourself — and what better way to do this than with an understanding and caring lover? That is a lover who can help you become intimate with yourself and allow you to open up and reveal your deepest feelings (the loving ones, and the ones which you most want to disown). Of course, you may not be able to do this overnight, but by taking a leap into the unknown (with the help of your pioneering spirit) you can make a start. Once you find your feet you will find intimacy easy, and you may find you are the first to tell all or reveal all to the lover(s!) in your life.

With a 1 in your chart you were born to lead, but that is not to say that you always enjoy it. For example, taking the lead in foreplay may be something you know you are good at but perhaps you do it to please the other person — not because you want to. Perhaps you instigate a relationship because your potential lover lacks the confidence to make the first move. You are working at finding your own direction in life and steering your own ship while you are the one carefully navigating the course. When a lover comes into sight on the horizon, or is on board, you may find yourself navigating for two, or you may like your lover to take the lead at times. Perhaps the man or woman in your life is forceful and directs you, which can be a thrill particularly in the heat of the moment, or at times when it seems like you have lost your sense of purpose or direction. You may even be searching for a father figure for a lover who can show you the way (or lead you astray!) where you may remain in childlike oblivion to whatever they say. Sometimes you may find you are 'led down the garden path' but this can teach you about life too.

The 1 influences you by making you aware of purpose in your life, and this may be reflected outwards with the lover you choose. 'Oh, I'll choose that lover because I can have children with him or her' or 'Another lover's better because he/she can improve my life by enriching my mind.' You may be very ambitious and may choose a lover who can help you fulfil your ambitions in other areas of your life, such as your career. Perhaps you may drift into relationship with a lover and allow yourself to be carried along with no exact purpose, except to live in the moment and make the most of each day. That is, you take the line of least resistance. You may also be so filled with purpose that you enthusiastically dive into a relationship with your lover(s) without thinking, and find they blow you away. However, if your lusty lover is expecting you to always drop everything to be at your beck and call, forget it, because you often focus your creativity into other areas in life – they are usually not the sole cause of your existence.

SEDUCTION, SEX AND AFFAIRS

You are often seduced with words, but you may like someone to come on strong so that you know where you are with them, because you can be so wrapped up in yourself that subtlety doesn't move you. You may not receive it as them coming on strong, but as a lover who is showing interest in the wonderful you. In your chat-up lines and in bed you can be so inventive that your lover sees you differently, as if in disguise, which can be exciting but also scary to some less-than-adventurous mates. You are also open to suggestion and you are usually willing to try anything once, so seduction techniques may need to be more than simply buying you a drink.

Within your primary relationship you may begin an affair to add a spark of newness to your life, particularly if your relationship has got stale in the bedroom. You may treasure the excitement of conquering a new lover, so a one-night stand may be just as exhilarating as the stimulation of a long term lover. You may also have affairs if your primary mate is demanding too much of you emotionally, or if you feel you have got too attached to him or her. On the other hand, if you are looking for intimacy and your primary mate can't provide you with that then an affair can help you access deeper feelings which you may be needing to explore. You can also be covert within your relationships, and you may go to great lengths to make sure that your partners never meet, or lead your primary partner in a different direction to avoid suspicion.

Sex is one of your favourite words, and you like a good work-out; it helps to release all your pent-up emotions and allows you to be creative with your energy. When you have learned to feel safe with your lover you really know how to let your hair down and enjoy the closest of sexual intimacy. Whether you are at home in, under or on top of the bed, or exploring the great outdoors, your aphrodisiac is inventiveness. You have mastered the art of surrender so that your lover can feel in charge, or you know how to go for your target and your goal of pleasure consumes your lover's goal. You may fear being taken over sexually and you may feel a victim sexually if you feel unable to assert yourself and say 'no', or 'not now'. You may fantasize about many lovers giving you pleasure and not needing to satisfy them (this is because you can be self-centred and seek only your own sexual fulfilment). Masturbation is a wonderful release for you when there are no lovers around, and you are generally matter-of-fact about sex and regard it as a simple and ordinary part of life.

FRIENDS

Friends can benefit from your company because you are outgoing, gregarious, vibrant, and you are able to energize them with your enthusiasm for life. For example, you may be very athletic which inspires them to take up some form of exercise to help them keep fit, or you may have a brilliant mind which inspires them to study interesting subjects. They may also admire your ability to find your own direction in life, or they may be inspired by your independence and your ability to look after yourself – your self-reliance. You love admiration because it boosts your feelings of self-worth and self-importance, and makes them feel good about themselves by you feeling admired too.

With the influence of the 1 you may prefer to have lots of different friends whom you can share your life with, like going to the movies, travelling on expeditions, educating yourselves on college courses so that you can share your intellectual interests together, and so on. You often prefer discussing current affairs to discussing your feelings (although your feelings about world events may come into these discussions too). Having lots of friends may mean that you do not necessarily need to get too intimate with any one of them emotionally. Having a best friend whom you can relate to and share all your feelings with may really help you though, because you tend to bottle up your feelings until you are fit to burst and they suddenly explode out of you. You like to set goals with your friends and you may understand why each person is in your life – to teach you to value yourself, for example, or you may have a joint goal of climbing Mount Everest together, and so on. However, you like to do things on your own too and even your closest friends may never get that close to you because you spend so much time on your own, which is your choice.

Your friends may also follow your lead because you have the ability to set trends, invent new ideas or useful things, or be the first person to do things a different way, and they may look to you for direction. Perhaps you set a fashion trend by designing or wearing clothes in your own unique way, and indeed you may compete to stand out in the crowd by doing, acting or saying things which set you aside from the rest. Perhaps you like to feel exclusive or detached. Some of your friends may also be strong individuals and trendsetters or revel confidently in their own uniqueness of being too, and so you can empower each other to be who you are.

With the 1 in your chart, you can sometimes lose your direction and get stuck in a rut, perhaps fearful of taking the first steps towards something or someone new. Your friends can be wonderful support at these times by helping to point you in the right direction or giving you words of encouragement about facing situations in life. The influence of the 1 means that you can be indirect and avoid dealing with problems that arise. You may even want your friends to rescue you. But where there is a problem there is a solution, and with your bright mind you are fully able to sort your own life out for yourself. You have an independent streak and sometimes being left alone is all that you need to get the energy to move forward with your life. Your friends have probably noticed that you are headstrong and wilful and, no matter what they say, you will do what you want in the end anyway!

FAMILY

You may or may not choose to get involved in family life. Perhaps you were an only child in which case you may have spent a lot of time with your parents (instead of with any brothers or sisters) or you may have spent a lot of time on your own. However, even when you did have plenty of family around as a child you would no doubt have been able to entertain yourself by turning to your creativity or to your studies or by inventing new toys and so on.

You are tremendously creative and part of your creativity may go into your relationships or creating children, or creating work and ideas, but for you there needs to be a creative goal in mind. If one of your goals is caring for your family, or being a part of a family, then you are committed. But if you choose to focus on other things then family contact may be limited. You are an independent person who is likely to move away from your immediate family on your quest for adventure and your pioneering can lead you far afield.

In terms of feeling safe to be intimate, particularly emotionally, family life can help you because these are often the closest people to you. Your cousins, other siblings, your parents or grandparents have probably seen you grow up, and therefore you may be able to open up to them or reach out to them more easily. If you were brought up in an environment where it wasn't 'done' to discuss your feelings, and that is OK with you, then you may also feel that your family are the safest people to be around. However, you can be self-centred by nature and even when your father, for example, is reaching out to you for love or help then you may not be fully aware of his feelings and may even be uncaring with your response.

You like to do your own thing and your family may be mesmerized by the life you have created, particularly if it is one which doesn't conform to their lifestyle or what society dictates. For example, if you have children you may choose to educate them yourself instead of sending them to school, or dress them in clothes other than the school uniform to bring out their individuality. You can also appear intimidating or shocking to others because of the path you take in life. This non-conformist attitude may exist, but at the end of the day with a 1 you may eventually do what you are told to do.

Your partner may also be challenged by your individuality because you want to do things in a certain way. You may be challenged by your partner's suggestions or feel threatened if he or she goes off and does things in the opposite way. Being part of a family or with your husband or wife challenges your individuality because you are being asked to consider everybody's needs. However, your caring and giving side also means that you like to make sure that everyone's needs are included within the family group. Interestingly enough, finding a group purpose with all your relatives can help you to lose your inhibitions and bring you out of yourself so that you can become more you, and therefore become even more of an individual. Getting involved with your family and your own partner or children's lives can give you a direction in life.

WORK RELATIONSHIPS

Whether you work from home, in an office or in a field, the most important aspect of your day is about being creative and fulfilling or achieving your goals. You are a goal-setter and with your dynamic will and ability to stay centred on your goals you often achieve them. Even when goals slip away you find other ones to quickly take their place. This makes you an easy person to deal with because you are clear about your intentions and your goals and straightforward about life.

As a boss you can set your team to work with your focus or goal in mind, and you inspire others with the energy you give to your work. Work is life for you because each day brings you something new, a new challenge, a new angle to look at life, and it can bring new goals too. You may expect a lot from your co-workers, and get angry or frustrated when they do not seem to make the same progress as you do. Sometimes your workmates may feel inferior to you because you have a way of seeming self-important or exclusive and above the rest, and also, because you can be detached and withdrawn, they may feel they can't relate to you. However, when you want you are good at getting others to see your point of view, and, even if they don't care for your creativity and your goals, they are very important to you.

With a 1 you explore many concepts in your mind and you then like to set about creating these ideas as part of your goals. You are an ideas person – a great quality for any business – and you are often easily able to find solutions to problems. You can invent new ways of looking at things or doing things which can profit everyone. People may notice how much you love being creative, and they may see you as an innovator, or someone they turn to when they need a push in the right direction with their work.

You are able to take the initiative and do not generally sit around waiting for others to tell you what to do. Unless, of course, you are fed up with showing others the way and enjoy a holiday by letting them lead you for a change. Sometimes you withdraw for long periods of time and work by yourself in isolation from others. If you work for yourself this may work really well, but if you work in an office with others relying on you as part of a team this withdrawal can be destructive. It can have a negative effect if you refuse to open the door to them and let them in. With a 1 you may prefer to work in isolation so much that your workmates may feel, even after many years, that they don't know much about you.

At times you may allow yourself to become so bogged down with work that it seems impossible to move forward with your life – in any direction. Perhaps you create this situation in order to avoid dealing with another aspect of your life. For example, perhaps you aren't happy at home so by taking on lots of work you can avoid facing the problem, or you may find yourself with a new boss or a new project and feel unable to express your feelings to anyone in your life and bottle things up. All relationships are important and by using your logical brain (as you do) you can find your own way of dealing with your relationships and life. You are an opportunist; your ambitions can mean that you wave the flag for new inventions to improve the world in which you live.

LOVERS

Romance is a key word if the number 2 is influencing your love life and what better way to experience this glow of affection and love than with a 2? Midnight walks along the moonlit beach, sumptuous dinners for two with candle-light and music serenading you, or even simple strolls in the park, are some of the beautiful scenes that could be awaiting for you. But whatever you do and wherever you go, hand in hand is the way you feel happiest. You like to hold hands because it helps you feel connected to your lover. When you and your lover touch you are transmitting energy from your lover to your hands and then to your heart (receiving) and you are sending out energy from your heart to your hands (giving) and on to your lover. This wonderful exchange of energies happens even when you don't touch one another but you like to feel close and for others to see that you are connected too.

One of your lessons in life is to learn about give and take, and your lover can help teach you about this in a wonderful way. You may be better at giving, and you love to do things for your lover, perhaps to feel more loved or because you want to please him or her. Or you may be better at receiving, and enjoy all the love and affection you often seek in a relationship and revel in your lover doing things for you. Sometimes you may find giving to another scary, particularly if you have been hurt in the past, because you may fear rejection. You can also feel equally scared by receiving, particularly if it is new to you because you have been in a relationship where you did most of the giving before. You and your lover are helping each other to heal parts of yourself and you attract to you just what you need right now.

You are also better at giving or receiving in different degrees with different lovers because you bring out different qualities in one another. You also find that you give more or take more at different times in your relationship, like when there are other external issues for you to focus on, or when you are going through a crisis or some intensely personal issues. Of course, when you give you receive, and when you receive you give. For example, financially, if your lover has been paying for all your wonderful weekend country breaks – he or she may love and get so much pleasure from being able to provide for you that you are giving him or her something wonderful too, in addition to the love and experiences you share together at your holiday retreat. When you give your lover a present like a red rose at breakfast you also receive yourself by seeing the look of love on his or her face, or by enjoying the love-in later. Giving and receiving, being receptive and active, yin and yang, is a natural part of life and with a 2 in your chart you are walking across a tightrope and learning how to operate this fine balancing act.

With the influence of the 2 you may be looking for equality in your choice of lover. Perhaps he lights your fire and you provide the body to 'burn'. This equality may also apply to your careers or you may choose a lover who can match your own place in the social scene too, and so on. Equality may also be important to you because you like to feel you are both playing an equal part – with equal responsibility – in creating your relationship. You may sulk or get moody if you feel your lover isn't pulling his or her weight and you may be only too aware at times when you are neglecting your lover's needs too. However, maintaining equality is challenging because it requires a lot of input and it can put great pressure on you both (particularly in the bedroom) to perform. Sometimes you give to one person and receive back from another which is one good reason to have more than one lover in your life if you so desire!

One of the shadow qualities of the 2 is that you can be demanding – and your lover can do no right when you are laying this on thick and fast. 'Yes, you must take me out to the movies now.' 'No, we can't make love until you've fed the cat immediately.' This demonstrates as the 1 wanting something from the other 1 (which makes 2!) right now. This push and pull may be a part of your relationship, but remember that the more you push the more your lover will pull, and vice versa. Meanwhile, you may be learning that the only way to achieve harmony and peace, which usually rides high on your list of priorities, is by learning to co-operate with your lover. Life is about give and take, and by compromising you can find happy solutions in order for you to move on with your relationship. So then you can lounge in the sun in your garden with your lover by your side, and relax knowing that the flowers are growing in their own time.

You are also learning to relate to people but you don't always choose the best time. For example, late at night when the love of your life is drifting into dreamland you may want him or her to discuss your essential feelings, and give you feedback and join in the discussion. By learning to be considerate and taking note of your lover's needs you can learn to choose a time when it is best for both of you to discuss burning issues. Learning to be mindful is part of what the number 2 energy is teaching you.

With a 2 influencing your love life you may be a gentle soul, who is easily pleased and who lives to love, and who loves life. You may wander through life searching for your perfect soulmate – a lover with whom you feel 'joined at the hip', and with whom you can feel the earth move. Or you may feel like every lover is your soulmate simply because they show you love and affection or are slushy romantics too – so then you feel they must be 'the one' for you. You are open to life and your lover may be able to read you like a book, but you make the decisions about which lover takes this special book to their heart or into your bedroom for romantic and cosy nights. Your intuition plays a part in deciding what is good for you. Sometimes you are as open and vulnerable as a tiny pup. You are highly sensitive to all your lover's feelings, as you experience your feelings deeply too. You like to feel supported by your lover and you are able to reach out your hand and support him or her through the good and the bad times together, because you like to share everything you do two by two.

Feeling separate is something which you may associate with being alone without a lover, and when you are not part of a pair it may feel very painful for you. You may cut off from your feelings or you may get over-emotional and intense. It's good to remember that the love of life is in the air you breathe and that love is all around you, and by breathing you can take in and give out this love which is there for you always. Learning to love yourself is important and by loving and honouring yourself, as part of life, you can learn to love others. This definitely includes giving and receiving love with a wonderful lover or your soulmate too. Life is simple, and by revelling in love you are contributing to the world in which you live in a positive way; love is what makes the world go around.

When you are centred you have a calming effect on your lover who may be attracted to you because of this inner peace which you seem to radiate out. He or she melts into our arms within your loving aura, as you share your sacred space together. Sometimes you may be too passive or placid and a lover who can stir up your passions may be just what your heart desires.

SEDUCTION, SEX AND AFFAIRS

In life there is only love and fear, so the perfect seduction for you may incorporate either. You may be seduced by affection when on your first date your potential lover feels comfortable to take your arm or your hand or showers you with kisses. Or you may be seduced by the thoughtfulness of your lover, or by him or her whispering sweet nothings in your ear. You love to feel loved, and the more you feel loved the more open you can be, and the sexier you feel. Fear can also seduce you, for example, having sex with your partner in a public place where someone may see you, or in a dangerous position (like up a tree or under water, and so on). You may be turned on by time pressure, putting pressure on your lover to perform, or by being pressurized (by others) that a lover is a *liaison dangereuse*.

In a primary relationship you may turn to an affair if you feel there is little emotional connection with your partner or if you feel the love has gone out of your relationship. You may seek these qualities in your lover, and enjoy sharing love-making sessions together. But you may find that working through your feelings about being in relationships with two people may be a challenge. Affairs can teach you about decision-making as you choose whether to keep your lover or your partner in your life, to balance your time with both, or to find someone new.

With a 2 in your chart (particularly if the 2 derives from an 11, when you can be very passionate and like to get carried away in the heat of the moment), you are likely to give all to keep your lover happy and to maintain a harmonious sex life. You love caring and sharing and what better way to do this than exchanging your vital energies in or out of the bedroom. You love to set the scene and make your environment as welcoming as possible so that the ambience feels good, looks good, and can nurture and support your intimacy with your lover. You love water, so the shower may be one place you love, or you may appear in a wet T-shirt or underwear for your lover and like the feel of it close to your skin. You may fantasize about making love with either of the sexes (exploring the duality of the 2). Or fantasize about making love with your brother or sister or family member (a real taboo which creates enough fear to stimulate your imagination). Tantric sex – operating your (sexual) energies to prolong love-making sessions, may also appeal to you. However, you may be just as happy to go along with a hug, a kiss, and sex twice a week under the sheets.

FRIENDS

You are a simple person who likes the simple life, and although you may be the first to offer a listening ear or a shoulder to cry on to any of your friends in distress, you generally like them to respect your need for peace. Indeed, if one friend seems to be taking up too much of your time you may avoid them for a while. This is because you are very sensitive to others' feelings and you feel their pain so deeply that you can easily take their emotions on and go off-balance. You can also knock them off-balance when you present them with a torrent of emotion and you can be challenging to them at times too. Of course, all your friends are teaching you something about life, and are teaching you to relate to yourself even when you or they are distressed.

Sometimes you can be a jolly anchor because of your peace-loving and placid nature and you can calm people down, and even when they are in the middle of a crisis you can help them to centre again. Perhaps they relate to your straightforwardness or your loving and caring attitude which makes them feel nurtured, loved, or emotionally secure. Relating through your emotions is necessary for you and your male and female friends may need to be ready for sharing the intimate details. Sometimes you hold back your feelings but your friends probably know when to dive in or to leave you alone, until you are ready to open up to them in your own time. You can also be needy at times and get overwhelmed by your emotions and demand your friends listen to you, but they are more likely to walk away if you are wallowing in emotion and leave you to sort out your feelings for yourself.

With a 2 influencing your friendships you may like to feel mutual support between you and your friends, and know that you can ring each other day or night and that you or they will always be there (particularly a best friend). However, sometimes you may rely on your friends' support too much and they may become a prop to keep you upright and you may become too dependent on them. Or you may spend more time supporting them than concentrating on living your own life. Emotions can be all-consuming (yours and theirs) and learning to find a balance by focusing on other things in your life may help you to stay centred.

You may feel fearful of getting involved in deep friendships, perhaps because you feel they will reject you, or they won't love you once they see who you are. But friends become friends because they love you the way you are; they know your gems of wisdom and beauty and they know your faults, and they still love you! And any quality about you which they dislike arises because you are mirroring back qualities within themselves that they are learning to transform too! Sometimes when you feel too close to a friend (perhaps you feel like you were too open and told them about something which made you feel vulnerable) you may try to get away, or distance yourself so that you can separate. But this is like running away from yourself. By being honest about your feelings with yourself, or with your friend, you are simply learning to love and be happy with the real you.

Talking and relating emotionally may be one way you enjoy relaxing and socializing with your friends, along with visits to yoga classes, listening to musical concerts, or going for a swim.

FAMILY

Family life is a natural part of your life as you love to relate to those who you are closest to. You may well have been brought up in a loving and caring home where you were nurtured and looked after, or it could be that you were called upon to do the caring for your family. Whenever there were problems you may have been the one to listen, or were you a little monkey and played your sister off against your brother, or mother against your father and got up to mischief? Perhaps you were the middle child, so that you could feel what it was like to have two other siblings to choose from, and maybe you didn't like playing piggy in the middle at all.

With the influence of the 2 you may dislike being in the middle of any situation where you need to take sides, particularly at home. This may be between your parents, or between your wife or husband and your children (such as in situations of divorce). You can be pretty uncompromising sometimes when you are put on the spot, and you may manipulate situations or people to avoid making direct decisions at times. However, you are open-hearted and, particularly with a divorce, you may well like to see both sides win and to come to some sort of amicable agreement. Indeed, divorce is one of the most painful facts of life; with a 2 it can seem unbearably painful because of the depth of your emotions.

Sometimes when there are family fracas and arguments – as there are particularly during get-togethers for special occasions – you may be called upon to negotiate a settlement in your own diplomatic way, which you may accomplish with ease. However, diplomacy isn't always your forte and you can be careless and hurtful with your comments and your actions when it suits you.

You may also show indifference to those close to you, perhaps because it is too painful to feel. But being indifferent to your family's emotions can cause chaos around you. For example, if your husband and mother-in-law (who lives with you) are reaching out for your help because they can't sort out their differences, then being indifferent to them may mean their intolerable situation worsens. This can create all kinds of challenges for you within your home environment. Co-operation at home can help to keep the peace and keep hearts happy too. Sharing and applying the wonderful wisdom and tolerance which are in your heart, can also help you and your family to face any situation in life, knowing that love always finds the way.

You often like to weigh up situations and measure yourself against other relatives. For example, your cousin passed her law degree with distinction and so you 'had to' do the same, and so on. This can create a lot of pressure (which you put on yourself), but this can also encourage you to do things you want to do. Perhaps you measure your children's development too, or even try to measure how much love your partner gives or takes from you. Weighing things up is a natural process for you whenever or wherever there is an equation of 2.

In your life instead of give and take you can think of sharing. Sharing yourself fully with your family means that they feel open to share themselves with you too.

WORK RELATIONSHIPS

You like to work in the best possible environment conducive to the type of work you perform. For example, hoovering your home can be considered work to you so you may do it with the music on or while listening to the television. Your physical environment, which includes all the people around you, is very important to you, and you may like it to be quiet or as harmonious as it can be. You may decorate your work space with plants or paint your walls with relaxing colours.

However, people are living and moving energies and they create a large part of the atmosphere in which you work. For example, if you are feeling emotional and are moody and snappy this will affect all your workmates, and why should they suffer? This makes your relationship with those at work really important to a sensitive soul like you. You may even leave a job, even with the best pay or position in the world, in order to find peace. Of course, peace is inside you and you take it everywhere you go. Another lesson you are learning is tolerance, but there is only so much you can take.

You like to share your work and to make sure it is shared in equal amounts. You are happy to help others with their work when they have too much on their plate and you like the idea of mutual co-operation. You can make a happy worker who placidly gets on with your job with no fuss or signs of protestation. However, on some days at work you really need close emotional contact and to relate to people in this way. On these days you love to spend your time discussing issues and problems of daily life with your workmates and spend little time working at all!

Perhaps you troll out to the pub or to a dinner with your colleagues to get down to more intimate conversation, and where you can enjoy eating and drinking – usually in moderation, of course.

People like you because you are open and approachable and you are able to listen to them without taking sides. You may be a very popular associate or form close friendships with the people with whom you work. You like helping people with their work and with their problems, and you like to feel people need you. But you are sensitive to your environment and sometimes feel hurt when you know they don't want you around. Feeling loved and needed at work helps you do a good day's work, and makes you feel good about yourself too.

With the influence of the 2 at work you may be challenged at times when you are called upon to make decisions, and you may prefer your colleagues to make them for you. For example, perhaps you are a designer and your company chief asks you which project you would like to take on. You may go into complete inertia waiting for someone to tell you what move to make next. Indecision can be quite a challenge for you and your company, particularly where time, money and reputation is all. But, scary as it is, indecision is one of the qualities you are working to transform.

With a 2 in your chart you may not like being average at anything particularly at your job, and you may always be weighing up your performance with those around you. However, you give all you can, and no doubt you can find some aspects in your life that really shine.

LOVERS

One of your essential ingredients, influenced by the 3 energy, is that you really know how to tell a good joke – 'Have you heard the one about . . .?' – and your hundreth joke is often as funny as the first! Laughter and humour play a large role in your life, you were probably born laughing at the midwife or pulling faces at her (you could make a living out of imitating people), and thinking, 'What a funny old world this is.' Better to laugh than to cry you believe. You have a wicked sense of humour that can get you into trouble sometimes, like when you are playing practical jokes on people. When you are in a bad mood your humour turns to ridicule and if your lover is the sensitive kind this may not be appreciated, or you may get a verbal slap in the face back. But you have the gift to make your lovers split their sides laughing, and laughter is the best therapy as it gets those little endorphines swimming around your body, helping to relieve your stress levels.

So you can see that your lover will need to be someone who has a sense of humour or who needs lightening up by being around you. You may drive them mad if you're like this all the time, like when you are fooling around playing the court jester and your lover is trying to talk to you about something serious, for example. You even handle serious problems with a pinch of salt because you just get on and deal with them instead of worrying too much about them or their consequences. However, your laid-back, carefree and happy-go-lucky attitude may mean that you sometimes fail to recognize what a potentially serious problem is, and this can land you in the middle of a landmine as you try desperately to unscrabble yourself from a situation (particularly with regard to relationships!).

With the influence of the 3 you can be rather emotional because of your sensitivity about life (which you may also try to cover up with laughter). Yes, you can laugh at yourself, but when the going gets tough, the tough get going, and if you feel yourself in too deep with your lover you may scatter your seeds elsewhere. You may do a quick turn to get out of the relationship if you have not found the perfect lover to tie you down, because you like your freedom. Or you may be flip with your lover or try to get your relationship onto a more superficial level (sex and tea, not dinner and sex), or poke fun at them to make them go away. You love to experience all the fun and lightness in life and you may prefer to express yourself with lots of different lovers and enjoy all the goodies which nature can provide.

You are learning about self-expression with this 3 energy, and one way you can do this is by constantly communicating to your lover. Much of your communication may be superficial because you may find revealing your true feelings too scary, but it all helps. This 3 may also influence you in the opposite way by being effusive, and a chatterbox, so that your lover finds it a challenge to keep up with you, or get underneath all the words to find out what your real feelings are. Can be tiring sometimes!

With a 3 you are basically a joyous person with a real ability to uplift your lover when he or she is feeling low, and your optimistic nature means you like to focus on the positive side of life. Your optimism means that with your lover (particularly at the beginning of your relationship) you may overlook their faults or potential incompatibilities; you may want to. When challenges do arise you may be surprised, but you often remain optimistic about sorting them out anyway.

You love socializing and entertaining people (not just with your sense of humour), and indeed you may spend more hours socializing than working. It is fortunate then that with a 3 in your chart you seem to have bags of energy and manage with little sleep (you may even need less sleep than other mortals around). No, it's not just because you've been up all night frolicking with your lover but because you are such an active person and you have so much to do that you'd rather be awake. Your lover may be attracted to you because of your gift for small talk and your ability to get along with people, and animals, and your culinary certificates (you usually have incredible talents here too). Unless they are the jealous kind in which case they won't like the serious attention you get all around. You seem to attract sociable lovers; they are on your menu too.

Your often bubbly nature means that you attract lovers to you like bees to a honey pot; except they may find it hard to stick to you. You're great at showing them how to let their hair down, and how to just let life flow (which can cause them great frustration particularly if they are organized and efficient and like everything to be done now). In fact, life for you may seem like a permanent holiday, with a drink in one hand, and a lusty, loving lover in the other. You just ease your way in to life and slip out again when you've had your fill.

On the surface you may appear a confident and outgoing person, but inside you sometimes fear you're no good at life, and doubt your abilities as a lover. Inside you may criticize yourself no end, and sometimes your inner lack of confidence means you project this criticism onto your lover too. This is another quality of the 3 which can be very exhausting for yourself and your lover. You may be a little devil and get your claws out. Imagine being told, 'You came too soon so you're no good at sex,' or 'I don't like your dress or the colour of your underwear tonight.' Great. Sometimes your mindsets play havoc with your confidence as you get so uptight with criticizing yourself for the lack of perfection in your life. Remember your lovely 3 is teaching you to let go and flow with life and if you are always picking fault then your lovers may go astray.

You are particularly drawn in and attracted to your lovers based on how they look, and you may even get caught up into believing that if they look good, then they must be good too. A supermodel or pin-up hunk may be wonderful to show around town at all the best parties, but what are they like in bed? Are they so busy posing in the bathroom mirror that they think you should surrender at their feet with no gyrating of hips or input from them? Can they hold an intelligent conversation about anything other than themselves? Do you identify with this too? Again your little angel of the day may inflate your ego but that's all they may do.

With a 3 in your chart you love a bit of gossip, or bragging about your latest lover to your friends, or even to the newspapers. You have a big mouth or you may choose to divulge vital information. Yes, 'Kiss and Tell' was probably invented by the 3, but watch out because loose talk can cost you your lover and your reputation. So if you are contemplating writing a sleazy novel about sex and vice, love and life, politics and all, then remember, although abundance reigns in your chart, money doesn't win you true friends. But it can win you instant see-through friends and a nasty headache if that is what you like.

You have a tempestuous nature and may dabble with many different lovers, being contrary at times about which one to choose. Or you may channel all your creativity into nest-making and a long-lasting, loving relationship with the lover of your dreams.

SEDUCTION, SEX AND AFFAIRS

You are seduced by physical appearance; big boobs, hunky shoulders, long legs, nice butt, or a seductive smile. But friendliness (very) can also seduce you. You invented flirting, and the way you win your lover over is to flash your eyelids, sink your eyes below their waist, tell a joke or two, and you become irresistible. Even if you possess an IQ of inhuman measure your animal instincts always seem to get the better of you, and you feel free to let your lover know what's on offer on the menu of the day. Another easy method to seduce you is by laying on the attention thick and fast (taking you to a party where there are lots of photographers will lend a hand), and will butter you up for the pudding afterwards. You are generally an easy-going person and if a potential lover puts up a fight you just can't be bothered.

With the 3, you may naturally be attracted to explore the 3 dynamic, and a primary partner plus a lover may seem the optimum solution. It may also make you feel very confused as your energies scatter between them both. You may take on a lover for some extra fun, if your primary relationship has got too serious or if they are very critical of you. Or you may need a lover to express yourself sexually if you are not connecting sexually with your partner. A lover may also be one way of getting you out of the door from a primary relationship, which you may feel is stifling your creativity and expansion.

With a 3 basically there is one motto regarding sex – 'Anywhere, anytime, anyone (well almost)'. This simply means with your casual, laid-back attitude you are happy to accept what the postman delivers on your doorstep each day. Your joy for life means you like to live in the moment and make the best of what comes your way. You are totally uninhibited, and group sex or three in a bed can be great, although voyeurism may be your forte too. You relish sex, and stripping off your clothes to reveal nature's gift may be your favourite pastime. You consider sex is natural, so even the most explicit sex or pornography may leave you unshocked. Perhaps you enjoy role playing as an aphrodisiac; the virgin or the whore, or dressing up in tantalizing body paints, clothes and jewellery to play the part. You know how to be rude with food, and your fantasies run wild. Your biggest fear may be only that you'll run out of steam. However, you can also be strictly moralistic too and believe love comes before sex.

71

FRIENDS

You are a freedom-loving person and you often make lots of friends on your travels. This is either as you literally travel around the world (which is one of your favourite occupations), or as you go about your journey in life. You are bright, enthusiastic and fun, and therefore your circle of friends is as likely to include anyone from a missionary from India to stars of the silver screen, with everything in between. You are adaptable to life and towards the people you meet, and you have an ease about you which means you can converse with anyone and about many things (often in a superficial way), which gets you by.

You are here one minute and gone the next and your friends know this. They understand you have wanderlust and they allow you your freedom, and perhaps they are freedom-loving too. But this can throw up challenges when your friends try to arrange to meet you for a social evening out. For example, you may be stepping off one plane and going on to another at the drop of a hat, and time has no bearing on you. Yes, you arranged to go to the movies with your friends but the opportunity came up to travel instead. Friends know to book you in advance (not that that means anything!) because your social diary can get so chocked up with invitations and events. Your popularity gains momentum as you go through life so it may be necessary to discard some 'friends' from time to time; you may return to some of them at a later date.

The 3 influence means that you may be more likely to have more friends of the opposite sex to your own. There are many reasons for this but animal magnetism is one of them. However, you may not like your friends to judge you on your looks alone (if this is an issue). Perhaps you expect them to see behind your looks or see through the superficial qualities, perhaps to the deeper mystical elements to you. You may be deeply religious or use your psychic or 'gut' instincts to guide you through life, or you may have an interest in spirituality. This doesn't mean you'll be flying off through the woods on your broomstick at midnight, but simply that you are aware of dimensions in life other than the purely physical.

Part of your popularity is naturally attributed to your sense of humour and you may love to chat with your friends about all the latest titbits and trivia from the daily press. You see the funny side to life and make up oodles of jokes about what you hear. When you gossip with friends about friends, no one is spared, and often your loyalty remains with whoever you are with at the time. However, your gossip is usually fun and entertaining and meant to be of no real harm to anyone. People often have a good laugh at you too with your wacky sense of humour, although you are sensitive to being laughed at or criticized and you may not like the tables being turned on you, not even in jest and when it is by your closest friends – who certainly know how to ruffle your feathers.

However, you don't sit on your butt gossiping all day, or loll around eating with them, because you are an active person. And aside from socializing you enjoy just as well jogging with them around the block, having a game of tennis, or going dancing together. You love action sport and can be a very physical person too.

FAMILY

You are a social person and social skills may be something which you were taught as a child, perhaps because you always had a lot of people around you or because your parents thought these skills essential for you. As a child you may have been infinitely creative and always making things or fiddling with your hands, or perhaps you had ants in your pants and constantly wriggled in and out of creative projects, sometimes without finishing them. Now you may be the type of person who hurries your food as you search for the next thing to do. Indeed, you can be easily distracted, and, particularly where family chores are concerned, you'd rather be out having fun. However, learning to focus on one thing at a time can be really useful to you.

You love socializing and so any excuse to throw a party is good for you; parents' anniversaries, children's birthdays, your cousin who passed his driving test, any occasion will do. You love to get close to your family and find out all their news, and you are the type to telephone them often to keep in touch, and go on joint outings with them. Food may play an important role in your life – perhaps you are a brilliant cook or you may simply enjoy eating. Indeed, heaven for you may be a meal with your family where you can eat and socialize with them too. Sometimes you turn to food when you are down, and at times eat everything in sight when you are feeling sensitive and emotional.

With the 3 influencing your family life you can be very generous, and you are the first to raise money by fund-raising for charity events for the less fortunate people of this world, particularly those with no food or no family.

You can be dedicated to working hard with your activities to help those in need wherever and whenever you can. You enjoy an abundance of laughter and usually a bounty of love in your life; these things are free, and you like to spread your joy around to all the members of your family and that includes material prosperity.

Futile arguments arise between yourself and your family easily because you can often be talking at cross purposes to them, or they dislike your superficial dismissal of issues which they are trying to raise. Sometimes you set the cat amongst the pigeons by baiting them with something that will wind them up, for entertainment purposes, or because you like a good argument. This may be a personal comment about the way someone looks or a criticism about them too. Rubbing your partner or your siblings up the wrong way may be one method of getting through your day but they also know how to get under your skin just as easily, and humour may be the only solution to the situation. Indeed, you are a master at diffusing situations and diffusing energy away from yourself, usually by focusing attention on something hilarious or by talking your way around situations. You have the gift of the gab, and the humour to be able to turn a war into a party.

Family commitments may sometimes bug you and resentment may creep in, particularly when you feel your efforts aren't being appreciated, and you're being criticized instead. You can also be hard on your children if you expect perfection of them. With a 3 you are a warm and loving parent and partner, and, as you're good with your hands, a relaxing massage from you is on the agenda too.

WORK RELATIONSHIPS

Life is a party to you and there's every reason why the merriment can continue at work too. For example, you may choose a job where you can interact or work with lots of different people you find stimulating. However, if your job requires you to sit at a desk all day and shut up you can handle this too, because you know that at lunchtime and in the evenings you can express yourself with those close to you. With the 3, sometimes you may enjoy the stillness of working alone, particularly when there is chaos going on around you, or in other areas of your life.

You like chatting but be aware that others may see you as a bit of an 'air head' as you don't even pause for breath sometimes between conversations. You may get too casual about the work you are doing because you are distracted by those around you, or because you are so busy on your mobile telephone organizing your social life and the next week's events. Sometimes you just don't pay enough attention or think through what you are doing at work and you may easily make mistakes. Of course, you make a joke of it, but you can only get away with it for so long. Tiredness may also be a challenge to your job as you spend late nights socializing and out on the tiles!

You are abundantly creative; you may paint, write, cook, do the gardening, massage, or use your creative time to study, and some of your creative projects may bring you great success. So whoever you work with, and however much time you spend chatting with your workmates, you may like to feel you have accomplished something at the end of the day. When you do work you are a real tryer, and you put in a great deal of effort which includes long hours – even if you are not generously paid.

With the influence of the 3 at work, you may have a casual air about you and sometimes your casual behaviour can get you noticed (particularly if you are caught indulging in carnal desire in the office or backroom), or by giving the come-on to your boss. You may not even notice when you are flirting much of the time because this is so natural to you. However, once again your sense of humour can help to get you out of a tight spot, and it may even brighten up somebody's day.

You like variety in your work and you are adaptable and able to carry out different tasks that come your way, which can be a real asset to yourself and to any business. Your flexibility means that you may get given lots of different projects to work on – you are very good at juggling and keeping all the balls spinning in the air at once. For example, if you are a receptionist (where you enjoy the social contact) you can handle the biker and the client on the phone while booking the boardroom for the colleague who is standing in front of you. On occasion the balls do fall down and make a dirty mess, and sometimes you have a habit of creating chaos and untidyness around you. But, life is for learning, and there is no point criticizing yourself for what comes naturally. You just get on up and go on, even if this does mean moving on to another job where your services and efforts are more appreciated. In general your fun-loving attitude makes you a popular workmate and your spark of joy can bring sunshine into what may be, for some, just another dull day at work.

LOVERS

With a 4, security is one of the most important issues for you in relationships. And as the feeling of security comes from within, then cultivating this by 'grounding' yourself in life is essential. Being grounded within yourself refers to your ability to feel comfortable and safe living within your environment; that includes your physical body and the physical world, as well as the whole environment in which you live. Grounding can also apply to your ability to deal with reality in a practical way, and to get on with life steadily, step-by-step. Therefore a lover who helps you to feel secure, helps you to keep your feet on the ground, and who nourishes your feelings of insecurity so that they melt away, may be very attractive to you. Naturally, you explore the passions of delight with your lover and this can make you feel real and good too. However, your lover can also feed your insecurity, for example, by not being committed to your relationship so that you never know when he or she is going to walk out the door. This may emphasize your responsibility to build your inner security by yourself, and the more secure you are perhaps the more your lover will feel comfortable enough to stay around.

Sometimes to test your security you take risks with

your lover, which may range from a marriage proposal to asking them to do something a bit out of the ordinary in the bedroom, and expose yourself to more insecurity in order to strengthen this characteristic. Sometimes risks pay off and other times they don't, but taking responsibility for your actions, whatever the results, can teach you to stay grounded.

Potential lovers may be attracted to you because they see good old Joe or Joanne Bloggs who seems ever so secure and comfortable and someone who simply gets on with life. Apart from the occasional dramas (which feed your insecurity too) they may see you as a solid person and someone who is surely dependable. Sometimes they see only the surface and envisage a comfortable but perhaps an unexciting relationship, or see a life of domesticity and routine in the future – even as a lover – as you beaver away at life. How wrong can they be! With a 4 in your chart you can be extremely romantic and passionate, and this 4 doesn't just relate to recreational sex but can also bring the influence of being a master of sexuality and that may take a lot of practice! This is because the 4 represents the earth and earthiness can be very sexy. Where the 4 energy means you may seem mundane at first, get to know you so that you feel secure and, hey presto! – watch out for the 'love bites'.

With the 4 influencing you then your ideal lover is someone who is also a good friend because friendship is one of the most important qualities which you look for within any relationship. And, once you have found your ideal friend and lover, then it may be a very short time before you are proposing to him or her, or making suggestions of a love nest together, and so on. Of course you would need to feel very secure with your lover to make this step, and you may prefer your lover to proposition you. Commitment can be a big turn-on for you, but, however deep you get stuck into your relationship and however steady it is, sworn allegiance is generally required.

Falling in love may be one of your fears with the influence of the 4, because floating around with your head in the air means that you are not grounded. And being ungrounded may spell disaster as far as you are concerned because once your daily routine – your survival mechanism – goes out of sync then you can feel very insecure. But imagine going through life and on your deathbed thinking, 'I've never been in love what have I missed?' Life is love and love is life and letting your hair down can be good for you – at least once in a lifetime. And if you do fall in love and you don't like it, then good, at least you've experienced another richness of life. 'But I'm much too practical to be in love' you think . . . imagine the passion and the fun you can have with your lover and you may just change your mind! And when your lover is in love with you that can make you feel very secure indeed!

You like to be able to get hold of reality and make it tangible, therefore, because you can't measure love or put it into a box, it may not seem real. Only your lover tickling your toes or putting a meal on the table seems real, or living together is real, but being in love is not. You may see love as what your lover can do for you practically and physically, rather than how intelligent, beautiful or spiritual they are – you look for the practical in everything. But with the romantic elements of the 4 you may also see beauty in every physical thing.

You like harmony in your life because it makes you feel secure when things are running smoothly, and if your lover is prone to dramas and major emotional upsets (like chronic PMT) then this may prove to be more than a challenge to you. Sometimes dramas can actually help to ground you, like when you are the one who is called upon to remain rock solid in a storm, and offer practical support when your lover is going off the rails. At other times you find conflict with your lover shakes your roots and your very foundations, which can be a big turn-off to you.

Occasionally you can be such an upstanding, responsible citizen that you feel the weight on your shoulders of your responsibilities and you may try to take responsibility for your lover too. For example, perhaps your lover didn't get his or her usual bonus this year, so you financially make it up to him or her. Or your lover hasn't got a home or a job so you materially sort that out too, or you pay for your holiday together in the sun, and so on. Well, responsibility usually comes so naturally to you that taking on a little more seems easy, but are you happy with that? Perhaps encouraging your lover to take responsibility for him- or herself can encourage you to do the same, so that you are both supporting yourselves in surviving in the physical world. Falling in love with someone principally because they do things for you may mean that you come in for a very sharp shock one day when they don't.

Sometimes you can get so bogged down in the practicalities of organizing your life with your lover that things get too serious and you miss out on all the fun things you could be doing together. Familiarity breeds contempt and boredom may set in. Instead of being predictable, like going out on just another date at the same old corner restaurant, add a touch of excitement to your relationship by being spontaneous from time to time. It can spice up your sex life when you are spontaneous with your love-making techniques or whereabouts you choose to make love.

You can be rather resistant to change, and even wearing differently coloured underwear may be challenging to you. Rigidity can lead to deadness as you lose connection with parts of yourself which then mirrors out as deadness in your relationships too. Sometimes you may need a bit of a push to try something new, and your lover may encourage you. Perhaps on a shopping date you may even take a risk and buy differently coloured underwear, shirts, skirts or make-up so that you can be flexible with your appearance. Being consciously creative can add a different dimension to your (love) life with your lover, and enhance your daily routine too.

SEDUCTION, SEX AND AFFAIRS

Security is the biggest turn-on for you, and you may be easily seduced by finding out that your potential lover has no one else in his or her life, has only had one relationship (which lasted many, many years), or that they have loyally been working for the same company all their working life. This suggests good potential to you – you believe that the person isn't going to jump in or out of your life, which would disturb your routine and contribute towards your insecurity. Friendship is also a big number in your book, and you are more likely to seduce a friend (or let your friend seduce you) because you feel comfortable with them – you know each other. But on occasion you can also be irresponsible, and wake up with a heavy hangover and no memory of how you got to be next to Sleeping Beauty, or what you did with him or her!

With a 4 you may begin an affair as a comfort blanket, to escape the monotony of your daily routine and responsibilities and to help you survive. You like to feel special, and if your partner has lost interest in you it may drive you elsewhere. Generally you will be secretive about your affair because anything that rocks the boat in your primary relationship and creates insecurity is no go. If you feel your responsibility in continuing the human race then you may go anywhere you can to fulfil this need; whether it is with your partner or your lover may not be an issue.

With the 4 influencing your sex life you are a very physical person and you may like to play rough and ready by biting or scratching your lover as you reach the heights of passion, or as an aphrodisiac. You need to feel safe and being firmly embraced, or feeling the firmness of your lover's physical contact, can help you to feel secure. You have an earthiness about you and you may like to keep your contact with the earth by having sex in the sand, in the hay, on the rug, or even perhaps standing up so that you can still feel the earth beneath your feet. You do like the earth to move, and you will go on and on to fully satisfy both you and your lover's sexual needs. If you are not looking to reproduce with your lover, then your biggest fear may be an unwanted pregnancy, and the fear of a condom breaking may bring you great insecurity. Birth control can be an issue. You may fantasize about being a sexy pin-up with the world's greatest lover who spends all his or her time pleasing your every need, and not having to work for a living!

FRIENDS

Loyalty is one of the qualities which the 4 energy influences, and if this number is in your chart then be prepared to work on this issue with your friends. You like to form solid friendships and to surround yourself with loyal friends so that no matter what challenges you face in life you know that they are always there, which makes you feel secure. Loyalty to you means being honourable and standing by someone and treating them with respect. You may have known many of your friends since childhood because once you have found a loyal friend you like to keep their friendship.

It can take you a long time to make true friends, but once you do, that's it, the bond is made, and loyalty is the game. Indeed if you find out that one of your friends has been disloyal towards you, just once, then you may be very black and white about it, and cut them out of your life just like that. When you are disloyal towards a friend you need to be prepared to take responsibility for the consequences; indeed you can dish out the dirt when you want to. With the influence of the 4 you may plod on through life with the same old friends because you resist change, and stay with the devil you know, rather than the devil you don't. Life may get dull at times – going to the same cinema, visiting the same friends – but routine may form the basis for your security.

You will do anything for your true friends and help them in any way that you can. For example, when they have locked themselves out you will drive miles to take them a duplicate key, or you will provide a bed for them if they're in the middle of a tricky relationship, and so on.

However, you are a person of structure and you like boundaries in your life, and for your friends to conform to them. Sometimes, you can even box your friends in. For example, you tell Laura, 'I can see you for brunch from 11.26 a.m. until 12.48 p.m., because I have a meeting from 12.50 p.m.,' or, 'I can't play basketball with you, Jake, because I always play with Sam on a Wednesday night, so Wednesday for the rest of my life is out of the question.' This takes boundaries to new limits! Sometimes you inflict such rigid restrictions on your friends that there is literally no space for them – or you – to grow, and they may choose to quietly disappear. Of course, you don't like to be boxed in too tightly either, even though you may like routine and compartments for everything and everyone in your life.

With a 4, when you feel heavy and you just don't know how you are going to get through another day, are worried about how you are going to survive, or you're feeling melancholy, your friends will let you know they're there. Of course learning to take responsibility for yourself, and learning to rely and depend upon yourself first and foremost is essential. But knowing your friends are there when you need them is very comforting to you.

When you feel secure it can enhance your friend's lives as well. For example, perhaps you have inherited a property from a rich uncle which gives you some added financial security, so you keep the property as an investment but typically keep an open house for your friends to stay there whenever they are around – which may be very popular with your friends who live out of town.

FAMILY

You as a human being have your own house or home which you live in which is called your physical body, and if you feel at home in it, relaxed and comfortable with it, then it provides you with the basis of security in your life. You may have been brought up in a large house by a wealthy family with all the material comforts you could have ever wanted but still felt insecure, perhaps sleeping with your bedroom light on at night. Or perhaps you were brought up with few material possessions but felt secure and happy in your childhood. Security is built from within, and feeling comfortable and secure in your childhood forms the foundations for the rest of your life.

With a 4 you may well find that you are part of a close-knit family, and that even if you are spread out in all four corners of the world then you still keep in touch, and visit them as often as you can. Loyalty to your family is expected before your friends (although with a 4 your family are often your closest friends), and your friends become part of your family too. This loyalty lends its hand to dropping all your business arrangements because a cousin is suddenly getting engaged, or if a relative is sick this can take priority over your personal life and all your arrangements. If you fail to turn up for a family christening or a funeral then it can be an unforgivable offence, and if you perform a deed of disloyalty towards one of your family members then it is always remembered.

Sometimes you may feel that you endure family life rather than enjoy it, as when you feel bogged down by too many family responsibilities. Fortunately your family are usually your friends and see when things get too much and may try to practically help you share the burden, for example, by looking after your two youngest children for the weekend so that you can have a break and devote more time and attention to your partner, or by providing you with food if you are out of work or have too many mouths to feed. Your family may also prey on you for financial support if you have plenty of money, and they may expect loyalty to constantly be extended by providing financial security for them too, which you may or may not choose to do.

You are a survivor, and no matter whether you have riches or rags you get on with your life and do the best you can. You are able to weather family dramas by being down to earth and practical and by keeping other areas of your life airtight. For example, at work you work, your personal life is personal, and home is for friends and family. These boundaries allow you to go to work no matter how much conflict there is at home or in your personal life and get on with the job without distraction. Similarly you don't take your work home (unless you work from home in which case your office is for talking work only), and so on. Boundaries help you manage family life and make you feel more secure.

One of your favourite family activities is to trace your family tree, or find out about your ancestors, because you know that they are the roots and the foundations of your family today. For example, you may find out about (and meet) your and your partner's relatives, so that your children, parents, or other siblings can feel more close and connected to each other physically.

WORK RELATIONSHIPS

With a 4 you like to work with your friends, which means you may set up a company with your friends, go and work for your friends at their company, or invite your friends to work at yours. It is more likely that you find work through word of mouth via your friends than in any other way. However, you can also make friends with your colleagues wherever you work, and work friendships are important to you. When you feel comfortable with the people in your work environment things are more relaxed, and work often becomes more enjoyable too.

You like to pull your weight and you take work responsibilities seriously. You also like to see everyone getting on with their own job and handling their own responsibilities. Sometimes people may try to dump extra work on you, because they are being lazy, or because they know you will persist in completing whatever work is given to you. You may take this work on because you fear losing your job and feel insecure, or you may do it because you think that you'll get promotion and extra financial benefits, or perhaps if you want to show your boss or other workmates just how much responsibility you can shoulder. Weights on your shoulder get heavier as you walk a long distance, and you have a tendency to take on more and more until you take a break, or are forced to. Sometimes your job may seem like an endurance test, as you exclaim, 'Just how much more can I take?' However, your friends at work, like you, are learning to take responsibility purely for themselves, and handling your own work responsibilities is plenty.

With a 4 you are a conscientious worker and you are

efficient, and organized too, and you are good at restructuring a system or a company when it is outmoded. If changes need to be made from the foundations up you may be called upon to help, and you really enjoy setting practical guidelines for your workmates to follow which can improve everybody's lives. You are well aware that when things are running smoothly at the grassroots level it helps everything else to run smoothly too. Sometimes when changes occur at work, for example your friend who sits beside you is made redundant, the change of routine can unsettle you for a while and cause great insecurity. You can be resistant to change, but change is a natural part of life that you need to learn to live with. Changes in your work environment can make you dig your heals in harder in order to hold onto your job; you dig deeper into the earth trying to find your roots and your security.

With a 4 there is an irresponsible streak influencing you which means you may do things at work which seem totally out of the ordinary. For example, you may forget to lock the front door when you were the last one out, or you may leave your job early without prior warning to go on a date, so that your company loses a contract or some business. You are not perfect and the pressures of responsibilities may mean you sometimes act in a funny, out-of-character way.

You may work for a lifetime at one career or for one business because, like your relationships with your friends, you seek long-term security. You are always thinking of ways in which you can make your future life more secure, and this includes your job and the people you work with.

LOVERS

With the number 5 influencing your love life then you are adept at change, and from one minute to the next your lover can be made aware of your many disguises. On some days you may seem talkative, bright and breezy, entertaining your lover by relating tales about your adventures in life. In the evening, you may be quiet, alluring and seductive, revealing yourself in your lowest neckline or your sexiest suit while your words manoeuvre you both towards the bedroom – to his or her place for the night. On another day, you may be sitting at lunch wearing the most casual of clothes, no make-up or aftershave here, while discussing serious politics with your lover. You are as changeable as the wind, and you need a lover who is adaptable to your ever-changing identity, and who can handle your different 'moods'. Your lover may need to be flexible too, and be prepared to go dancing, visit an opera, or go on a midnight hike around your nearest woods, all at a moment's notice.

One of the challenges for any of your lovers (lovers plural because you live life at such a rate of knots that you may have been known to change lovers as often as your clothes), is that you say 'Yes' when you mean 'No' and vice versa. Or you sometimes don't make firm commitments at all. Yes, there are some dates you do turn up for – often late – but even if you have booked a table in one eaterie then you may be getting up and going somewhere else as soon as you arrive. What definite advantages there are to dating you is that, influenced by this changeable 5 energy, your lovers will certainly learn to live in the moment as they try to keep up with you.

With a 5 you are bursting with life and you like to leave no stone unturned. You have the potential to say, when you are dying, 'I tried everything in life!' You not only tried but dived in head first. Yes, you are a wanderer and an adventurer and if your lover likes bungee jumping (with you both tied together in safe embrace) or tightrope walking across the Seine – great. You are a dare-devil who often takes risks for the thrill of them, so that you feel really alive. And, while your lover can stand and watch you perform, it's much more fun when there's two of you (particularly in the bedroom).

While many people fear change, wrestle with change, or try to avoid change, with a 5 in your chart you revel in it. You love the excitement of not knowing what is just around the corner, or what surprises are going to come your way. Indeed, if the man or the woman of the moment tells you they've bought you a gift, you may say 'Give it to me later' as you like the suspense – or you may get cross if they reveal what it is before you've had a chance to unwrap it. You like to surprise people too by sheer force of your personality, and if you attract a lover whose life seems a little boring then you may be just the person to give them a good shake-up.

Each lover in your life is a real adventure, and the way

he or she smells, the way they talk, the way they look, their mannerisms, how their mind works, everything about them intrigues you. However, you can be intense in your attentions towards your lover, but there needs to be more than good manners in bed to keep you interested, as boredom is enemy number one. Sometimes you may get too intense for your lover – all that attention is just too much for them – and they back away from you to get some space. You like a lover who appears a little mysterious, a little different from the rest, and somebody who may be considered eccentric could be your best bet. Your lovers are usually hopelessly mesmerized by your sexual magnetism and all your charms, and by your infectious sense of dry humour which can keep them laughing all night long. You are witty and bright, and a fine conversationalist when it is called for and the occasion is right.

With a 5 in your chart you love the freedom to express yourself and you love the challenge of exploring as much as you can about relationships and about life. If a lover tries to tie you down to commitments you may be 'off and on' with them, or pick up your suitcase and go travelling for months on end to avoid making commitments. However, long-term relationships are still for you, because a lover can teach you about life, particularly if they have some kind of master mind. You may choose a lover who knows how to keep you on your toes, so that the mystery of never quite knowing them is like a ball of string to a young kitten. Once a lover has got you hooked, and if they are absolutely fascinating or drop-dead gorgeous, then you may do the running after them instead; toodle-oo! Indeed, addiction is another quality influenced by the 5 and they may become your latest one.

Restlessness means that you can hardly sit still some-times, and even when you have found a fabulous lover your itchy feet may get the better of you. Promiscuity may be one answer, but learning restraint and to fully experience the relationship you are in with your lover right now may mean you feel more fulfilled at the end of the day. At other times you are a notorious flirt and you restrict yourself so much that admiring potential lovers with their clothes on may be as far as you allow yourself to go. Or you may restrict yourself to one lover, even when the love-ins are not that great – because you fear the change of moving on.

You are a sensual person and you are very aware of your body; you walk with your head up, and you carry yourself well. You have social etiquette too, and your lover can take you to any social occasion and be proud of you. Except, that is, on occasions when you've drunk too much of the hard stuff, or when you've really gone over the top by trying to pick up the other hot stuff around. Trying to pick up your lover's best friend in front of him or her may give you an adrenalin rush, but it may abuse your lover's generosity too. You like to communicate what you think, and if your lover reprimands you, then stopping to think before you speak may prevent you upsetting the apple cart and revealing truths. You can be too tricky for your lover to handle at times, but then karma comes along and much to your dismay you can find yourself embedded with a tricky lover too.

You like to know all the facts about your lover, and you are so inquisitive that you may interrogate him or her, such is your thirst for knowledge about people and about life. This may be flattering for a while, but tiresome when the questions never end. You feel free to let them know all about what makes you tick, but it may not be until after they have told you their life story first. If you are sceptical that your lover does not live up to their self-portrait then you may restrict what information you reveal to them about yourself, and just feed them titbits to tease them instead. Communication is important to you and you like a two-way dialogue, but you may prefer to communicate with your lover in other ways, sexually for example.

With the 5 in your chart you may be volatile towards your lover from time to time, perhaps because of the intensity of a passionate relationship, or because you feel too involved or too committed to your lover and you feel trapped with no escape route. Sometimes your intuition gets you out of situations, like learning to stay in your relationship, by giving you a clue as to how you can work things out.

SEDUCTION, SEX AND AFFAIRS

A potential lover may seduce you by offering you the opportunity of the adventure of your lifetime by taking you a) for a ride in their speedy sports car at midnight, b) to a safari where you camp out in the middle of all the dangerous animals and where you can make love in the heat of the night, or c) go on the world's tallest merry-go-round that turns you at 360 degrees, with them by your side – and so it goes on from A to Z. Once they set the wheels of your mind in motion you may simply fall into their arms as you get whisked away. Brains and an Oxford or Cambridge First may also impress you, or an aristocrat who has the money and the time to spend (on you) may do the trick. To seduce a potential lover you may simply lay all your attention on them, and hold on to every little word they have to say.

When you are in a primary relationship you may find a lover adds a spark of excitement to your life, particularly if that spark has gone from your day-to-day living with your partner. Perhaps you start an affair because it is risky, and the fact that you might get caught out can turn you on. If your partner tries to restrict your freedom in the relationship by making demands then an affair is one way of making sure *you* know that you are still footloose and fancy free. Of course an affair may just seem like one big adventure, and bring you the stimulation of change.

The element of surprise is a big turn-on for you in your sex life, so finding a willing lover who is willing to be oh-so-adaptable and adventurous is essential; a quiet mouse may not be quite your ideal! You love to tease and taunt, and one of your favourite aphrodisiacs is your ability to tell raunchy, hot 'n' spicy sexy jokes. Talking dirty can be a turn-on for you too – you may love to be vulgar and verbal. You like spontaneity and you may be uninhibited and perform all kinds of sex work-outs with your lovers. You like to shock, and sliding down steep ski-slopes with your lover in tow in the nude may be the kind of dare you'd go for. Or you get a buzz from performing the sixty-four positions of the Kama Sutra in the snow to a stimulated crowd of onlookers, or by getting pulled up by local security and told to get your clothes on. However with a 5 you remain largely unshockable. Being so wild and open at times you may fear being taken sexually advantage of, or in the extreme this may even be your fantasy. You love to experiment and finding out what your lovers like may be just the experience you need.

FRIENDS

If you have a 5 in your chart then you may see everyone in the big, wide world as your friend, because everyone is a part of your adventure in life and has something interesting to share with you. However, once you have discovered some new jewel of a friend, your friendships may burn out very quickly as you intensely want to find out all about them, and to be with them perhaps every minute of the day. And once you have fulfilled your needs, you may move on to the next jewel in the crown. Sometimes what you see on the surface with a new-found friend isn't how you see them weeks or later down the line, but you're wiser from spending time with them. Of course, some of your friends don't like being picked up and put down again according to your whims, and may feel abused by this kind of behaviour, but you are not perfect, and like everyone else you are learning about life by experience.

Anyway, you may be fickle and blow hot and cold, but there are some friends who do manage to stay around for a lifetime. Perhaps these friends know how to keep you entertained, or they may share the same attitude as you by living life to the full and putting in effort to make the most of each day. Indeed, you share a particular affinity with these 'blood brothers', as you all feel free to be yourselves with each other and to explore life.

One of the more destructive experiments you may explore with your friends is using drugs to give you an artificial high, so that you can have adventures of another kind. Perhaps you turn to drugs when there seems to be no other adventure around, and life seems to be going around and around. You may get addicted to drugs and hang out with others who support you with this habit, until you realize it ain't that cool, and move on to something new. Perhaps you get addicted to alcohol and find friends to experiment with that too. Addictions are a part of life, although they can be dangerous and your 'A Team' friends may encourage you to get addicted to laughing or something positive instead. Life is a gamble you think, and although you are not necessarily the type to sit at home waiting for your friends to ring you, your phone can be very busy. You get up and go out into the world, live your life, and take your chances.

Sometimes, just sometimes, you like to take a rest from talking, doing and meeting people, and you may retire for an exotic massage from one of your friends. You are only too happy to return the compliment, and you are very sensual and intuitively know where to put your hands even if you're not trained. Perhaps you feel telepathically connected with your friend and you know just where they want you to massage. It is in these moments of stillness that you experience the most clarity about your life, like when you are seeing a beautiful landscape or eating watermelon and everything is clear and bright – just like you sometimes.

You may be challenging to your friends by rarely being available because you are so popular, but when they do see you they appreciate your wonderful lightness and your sense of fun and excitement which lights up their lives. And all your friends can add to the richness of your life by sharing themselves with you.

FAMILY

Life is exciting and when it isn't you can become very restless and want to walk straight out of the door. For example, as a child you may have run away from home for some adventure and excitement, or to get attention, or because you were fed up with your daily routine. Perhaps you were difficult to please because whatever friends or family you had around, you were always looking for more of a thrill and excitement elsewhere. However, restlessness and boredom as a result of your insatiable need for stimulation (both mental and physical), is one of your major challenges in life.

With a 5 you are a communicator and you love to talk merrily away with your relatives about what is going on in the world, or help them to get clarity about problems in their life. Your relatives can help you to sort out your confusion about which way to go forward, and you, in turn, can offer them some plain, commonsense advice. You are very perceptive and you have the ability to see deeper than meets the eye, and if your family needs intuitive guidance they may look to you to provide it. When your relatives are sick or in need of some light frivolity you will happily sing and dance if it makes them feel better and if it helps to bring them back to life. Perhaps you spring some naughty jokes on them to cheer them up, or let them hear just one earful of you singing in the bath which is enough to make them split their sides laughing – you may even be a professional singer.

With a 5 influencing your family relationships you can make a wonderful parent because you have a bright mind, a quick-witted sense of humour, and a sensual connection with the earth. You are happy to educate your children to feel free to express themselves in all areas of their lives. Children take to you because you are fun and happy to be with, and they can tell with you when enough is enough.

Sometimes your lack of commitment can be destructive, particularly in your relationship with your partner because it means that when you aren't committed the partnership can't go as deep or as far as it would if you put both feet firmly on the ground. Of course that's OK if it's what you want. You may like trolling off out into the world for adventure without him or her in tow, so you can experience your freedom. If your partner tries to restrict your movements or wants to know what you've been up to when you were out, forget it. On the other hand, perhaps you have learned to find freedom in your commitments to your partner, and by each of you respecting the other's needs. However, with a 5 in your chart you can be unpredictable and you may order the wedding dress, but at the last minute get cold feet and fail to turn up at the altar, or postpone your wedding to a later date when you are ready to take the plunge.

With a 5 you live an exciting, action-packed life, roaming around the world having fun, and communicating to all and sundry along the way. You may often travel with your partner and children but sometimes you like to escape family life by setting off with the wind in your hair as it takes you off in any direction it blows. Therefore your family's needs may sometimes be neglected as you set off in search of yet another adventure.

WORK RELATIONSHIPS

You are learning to communicate with people and with the world, therefore you will probably work in an environment which allows you contact with others in order to be able to explore this aspect of yourself. For example you may work in the communications field, and make your living from communicating with people on the telephone, in person, or via computers all around the world; you are a people person. Even the most mundane jobs get easier when there is someone there to communicate with while you are carrying them through. You are generally very clear in your communication and therefore instructing your workmates may be something which comes naturally to you. Perhaps you instruct them on how to use a computer, or how to handle a difficult customer, and this can be very helpful.

You have a gift for perception and whenever you notice a job not being carried out to its best potential as a result of a lack of communication you may step in. Of course, you can be pushy and dive into situations where you are not welcome, just because you think you know what needs to be said. You can even make bad situations worse by deliberately stirring up comments made by work colleagues and communicating them in the wrong direction. However, you are generally a positive person and you can be a wonderful messenger who communicates knowledge out to the world in a positive way too.

Sometimes you speak without thinking and innocently put your foot right in it by speaking out about things which need to be kept under wraps. You are also good at exposing trade secrets which you think need to come out in the open for the benefit of everyone – to show the facts as they are. The sceptical and sometimes deceptive qualities that the 5 brings may mean that your work colleagues are a little hesitant or wary of you, but they warm to you when you are in a fun loving light-hearted mood.

At work you are very keen to learn, and even when you think you know your job inside out you will explore even more to try to discover new dimensions. When you discover new ways of doing things, it gives you a buzz. You love change, and doing the same job every day may bore you stiff without the added stimulation from all the people around you. You have a strong intuition and a scientific brain which likes to work things out and you may like to see the proof of the pudding. For example, if Harry your work colleague tries to sell you a new product, you may refuse to take it on face value, and test it for yourself to make sure it's in running order before you make your purchase.

At work you are as likely to spend your time flitting off to the canteen for a coffee to discuss the details of last night's adventures in the small hours as you are to be working hard at your job. You love to feel alive, and exchanging all the latest news with your friends at work can be light relief to you. When you get restless with your job and you impulsively want to walk out then and there, having added distractions from your friends and a giddy half an hour may really save the day. Commitment is one of your major challenges and if you do flip from job to job seeking change, then at least you learn a little more about life, and meet some interesting people along the way.

LOVERS

You like choice, and right from your first date with your
lover – where you go, what you eat, and so on – you like
to feel that you have the right to choose. For example, if
your lover booked a table at a restaurant without con-
sulting you then it may put you off them because he or she
is trying to make decisions for you. Of course, choosing a
lover may be a challenge to you with so many admirers
lining up to escort you into their arms and into their
hearts. And because you are an idealist and have very
high requirements and sometimes unrealistic expectations
about how your lover should match up, then the choice
can be difficult. Sometimes you can be too choosy, or
waiver for ages, weighing things up as you try to decide
whether you have made the right choice when you are in
the relationship. Even when you have found your ideal
lover you like to feel that they are not the only one, and
that there is still plenty of choice around in terms of
available lovers at any given time should you change your
mind. However, you will happily let your lover know that
they are the special one who has captured your heart, and
you know that you are their choice too.

You are highly romantic and a drive with your lover in

an open-topped classic car through the country on a hot day, with your chequered tablecloth, a bottle of wine and a basket full of goodies, may be your ideal way to spend an afternoon. You love to feel the warmth of the sun on your skin and your lover's body heat makes you feel loved and secure. Romantic picnics for two, and romantic dates are always welcome with you, and feeling close to your partner emotionally can be as important to you as getting close under the sheets. You fill your life with big bear hugs and kisses, and lots of loving affection too, and a straight-in and straight-out lover who has no time for love may not appeal to your sensitive nature. And if your lover is lucky enough to stay in your life then swearing and cursing in front of you, and any kind of vulgarity, may be quite out of the question.

With a 6 in your chart you like to feel loved and needed in your relationships, and even if your lover is a temporary visitor you still search for the feeling of emotional connection with them. So sharing your feelings with your first-time lover and going out with them on a few dates before you allow him or her to get next to you may be essential. With a 6 you like to feel good about yourself and your lover, and you like to look attractive; you will take a lot of care over your appearance and expect your lover to make the effort too. Of course, with a new lover you are going to make a special effort to look trim, but you take care of your appearance anyway. If your lover turned up for date after date looking unkempt then your instincts may lead you elsewhere.

Sometimes when you have a long-term lover they may help to smash your illusions of idealism and glamour (particularly if they are normally the model type) by refusing to match up to your standards. And, as they say, if you care for a person anyway then it doesn't matter what they wear, because it is who they are underneath that counts. Of course, you are a loving and caring person, and at the end of the day, love is what matters. Indeed you can be openly generous with your love, but at times you take to smothering your lover with too much love, kisses and affection. You like to nurture your lover and from the moment he or she wakes up in the morning you are there to please.

Giving to your lover makes you feel needed especially when they say to you, 'How could I ever have lived before without you in my life?', which they would say if you were loving, feeding and nurturing them every time they are in your presence. Sometimes resentment creeps in, like when it feels you are the only one constantly flexing the 'give' muscle while your lover simply receives. However, with a 6 in your chart you are learning about service, and perhaps your lover is helping to teach you just that. But in an ideal world perhaps you'll attract a lover who'll devote all his or her time to you too.

With the influence of the 6, you often surrender to your heart and leave your head behind, so if taking the morning-after pill isn't on your agenda then casting a glance at the situation before you get in too deep may be necessary. Sometimes you like to get stuck into your lover, and get involved in his or her life and end up trying to take on their responsibilities – to the extent that you can get carried away with theirs and forget your own. Perhaps your lover draws you in because he or she knows you are good at seeing the whole picture and can help heal the situation they are in. But you are also part of their scene too, and helping to heal them is also helping to transform and heal other parts of you.

You are generally a 'nice' person and you like to think that your lover sees you as a nice person too, so you will do what you can to make sure that this image is not shattered and that you appear like a little angel. Sometimes you get so carried away being nice that you bottle things up, because being horrible or getting angry with your lover seems too much like self-indulgence, and it's just not fair on him or her. And if for some reason your lover's not nice to you it can really throw you because you are such a nice person that people can't possibly think of being otherwise to you! But being nice all the time isn't real either and you can place too high an expectation on yourself to be all 'apple pie' because you like to behave perfectly with your lover. To be yourself and a real person you can't always go around with a smile on your face, smelling of roses, and looking all neat. And if you can let your hair down with your lover by allowing yourself to be real and express yourself when you are feeling something deep, then it can open you up to an even more loving space inside. Feeling at ease and relaxed with yourself will pervade your lover's life too.

With a 6 you love luxury, and you may be very attracted to a lover who can afford to take you on a long, lingering, luxury cruise, or who buys you champagne and caviar, or delicious and delightful underwear, the finest lingerie around. You love all the sensual delights too, like a lover who dangles luscious grapes into your mouth as you lie on a thick rug, or rubs you endlessly with sweet-smelling jasmine oil or something that pleases. You are like a pussycat with your lover. You love dogs too, and you follow your animal instincts in pleasing your lover and making him or her feel real good. Wearing smooth silks or rough leather all day and night long, particularly when your lover's around, may be one way to please, or placing thick fake fur on your bed or as a carpet lying open and inviting on the ground, which you sink in to when you've both got love in mind.

With a 6 in your chart you are likely to fall prey to a broken heart at least once in your lifetime because you fall in love easily and totally, and with gay abandon give your whole heart. But you love being in love, and love to love, and may choose another lover to share your heart. You can be a heartbreaker too, as you casually turn many lovers away, even though they worship you or pursue your attentions. Sometimes you attract jealousy as not all lovers like the competition floating around you all the time. You may have also learned to scratch too by being venomously jealous when your lover abandons you for someone new.

SEDUCTION, SEX AND AFFAIRS

Being a sensual and essentially romantic kind of person you can be seduced by the attentions and powerful emotions of desire from a potential lover, or simply by them presenting you with flowers or chocolates, or by reciting romantic poetry (yes, on your first date!). And if 'butter wouldn't melt in your mouth' then sometimes a little of the opposite coarse behaviour from your lover may also seduce you (as you blush). Perhaps you like your lover to carry you away (literally) and to 'sink his or her teeth into you' by giving you oodles of affection and loving kindness. With your instincts running high you may feel your way into your potential lover's life by encouraging him or her to feel you – by touching you or by sharing his or her feelings with you, so they feel open to you.

With a 6 you are keen on a monogomous relationship and one reason for an affair may be to get your own back on your partner if they have broken that commitment. When you're hurt you can be so vindictive that your partner may feel like moving home or country to escape from you. If your partner has been unfaithful you are likely to parade your lover right in front of their nose, or jealously communicate all the details of your affair. However devoted you are to your partner, the allure of the glamour of an affair and the opportunity to exploit your animal instincts can render any attempts at self-restraint as futile.

When 6 is influencing your sex life then you know that mastering your instincts is going to drive you on in pursuit of passion and pleasure. 'Needs must when the devil drives,' and if in your daily life you can never get enough sex and passion then taking on more than one lover (at once) may be your answer. However, kissing is like sex to you – it's your aphrodisiac – and it can help towards satisfying your daily desires. You love to feel good and making love after a romantic meal is heaven to you, particularly if your lover is a dream lover too. You may scent the sheets with perfume or simply be driven wild by the natural smell of your lover's body. With a 6 you may fantasize about being a professional sex thera-pist. You have an open heart and a devotion to service; you are skilled in love techniques too. Sometimes you can also get obsessed with sex and with fulfilling your desires and no matter how much sex you have it is never enough. Turning towards your heart and love may be the solution.

FRIENDS

With a 6 in your chart getting together with a group of friends for a meal or to dance or simply to chat is your ideal, because you like to do things in groups. A group is bigger than me or you because it expands out into your community. A group accounts for all tastes and styles and a group is where everyone can play their part and in an ideal world fit into. And the wonderful thing about being in a group is that if one person drops out of your group of friends, or three more people join in, it makes no difference because it is still a group. Sometimes you may find yourself going out for years with a group of friends who all do the same thing and suddenly just one new person joining in changes the group dynamic and can lead you off in a different direction. Each person is unique, which is why you find being involved with a group, or different groups of friends, very rewarding indeed.

You are a warm and caring person and any time your friends want to drop in on you they can because your door is open wide. You are welcoming to your friends and they are often happy to oblige you. You are good at listening to them when they have a problem they want to talk over, and indeed you seem to play the agony aunt or uncle to everyone in your group. You are very sensitive and you can really feel their problems and pain, but sometimes you get fed up with listening to them go on and on about the same old thing over and over again. However, you need to feel needed and by helping others you get this need met, but you can see that when you are serving others, then they are serving you in some way too.

With a 6 in your chart from time to time you can smother your friends with love and affection so much that they feel like they are going to suffocate, but you may do this because you love them so and want them to feel loved too. But you may also be smothering them because you think that this will make them love you more. You are very sensitive and if you feel rejected by your friends you sometimes retort to sarcastic comments, or acid behaviour to punish them, and make life difficult for them. You can certainly be awkward when you want, as much as you can turn on the charm to placate a friend who is angry with you.

'Music is the food of life,' and feeds the soul, and with a 6 you may like to hear the sound of music wherever you go. Of course birds make music, and the sea, and dolphins too, and all of nature's sounds can happily entertain you. No doubt some of your friends also share your enthusiasm. Perhaps your friends are arty or fashion-conscious like you, or are interested in law and order and in the justice system. With a 6 in your chart you have a love of beauty, and you appreciate the beauty and the wisdom within all your group of friends.

You may like to stand out from the crowd and constantly find yourself weighing yourself up against your friends. For example, perhaps you think they look more attractive, have a better singing voice, are more popular than you, and so on. Until, that is, somebody points out that they think you are better at cooking than them. Each of the friends in your group are unique and special in their own way, and that includes you, and you can see all the wonderful people in your group contribute to the whole.

FAMILY

You may expect your partner to spoil you with love because you were spoiled as a child. Indeed your parents may have idolized you, or made you feel so perfect that you felt 'top of the class' or let you get away with things easily. Perhaps you were the youngest child – the baby of the family often gets spoiled – or perhaps you were an only child. Of course, this may have caused jealousy between you and the rest of your family – if you always got served the largest portion of chocolate cake or were given more money for your birthday present, and so on. Being spoiled by your family may mean that you have an expectation that the rest of the world needs to deliver the same goods, and you may have been in for a little surprise.

However, you are a loving and caring person and you seem to give your love generously and naturally. You often feel deep compassion for all your family. Sometimes you feel this deep contentment from feeling so much love, and on occasion you may feel so overwhelmed with your family responsibilities that you wish you were free to enjoy life on your own without the constraints of family duties. Sometimes you feel guilty for not doing enough for your family, but you can only do what you can do. When you have arguments or family feuds, they can be longstanding as you constantly remind them about 'just what they did to you,' and blame them rather than taking responsibility for your part in the equation. Indeed you never forget when someone has been unfair to you because you like to see justice done. However, if any of your family members have arguments with outsiders then you are the first to stand up and defend them too.

With a 6 influencing you marriage, children or commitment within relationships are very important to you, and you will do your best to find a partner to whom you can commit. One of the most challenging situations you may face is when you are in a long-term relationship and your partner will not make the final commitment, that is, whether to live with you, marry you or whether to have children with you. But consider your partner may be mirroring something in you.

Sometimes you may approach your commitments like you approach sex; you may take a long time with the warm-up, and simply enjoy all the hugs and kisses before the climax. You are a nest-builder and you like to provide all the love and the emotional security for your family. With your love of beauty you fill your home with beautiful objects and colour it in lovely designs. There may be a real sense of community spirit in your home as you like all your extended family to regularly drop by. You may also organize community events for your family and you enjoy your place in society. However, at times your family plays such a large part in your social life that you rarely need, or have time, to socialize with anyone else.

With the influence of the 6 you can be sloppy, romantic and sentimental with your partner and your family too. Perhaps you save invites from parties you attended together, or keep your family albums so well stocked with photographs that they are bursting at the seams. Perhaps you sentimentally hold on to your child's school uniform which is now outgrown. You are a sensitive soul, and you may also be a hoarder of the past.

WORK RELATIONSHIPS

You are a team player and if you are the head of that team you expect every member to pull their weight; you will not tolerate five people doing all the work while one person sits by and drinks coffee all day. You like everyone to know which cog they play in the group, and you like to make sure that everyone in the team fully understands their role, so that they can get on with their own jobs. Indeed, if a worker doesn't understand their job or the project they are working on, you have the ability to turn it around for them to let them see it in another light. You make a brilliant manager because you can see the whole picture and what needs to be done. Even if your title isn't manager you may be naturally treated like one as you assume this position without thinking, or you may be elected one by the people you work with.

You are group-orientated and you tend to get along with many different types of people and fit into many different groups. For example, you get on with the management and your clients and the junior with the same easy manner that you have with your friends. With a 6 you may seem to be something of a communitarian as you are interested in everyone's welfare, and in helping your local community, for example, by fund-raising for charity. You have a social conscience. Your work colleagues warm to you because you have a big heart and are always willing to help when they come to you in need.

With a 6 in your chart you like to feel part of the team, and you may also love the attention of being an outstanding member of that team too, like winning some accolade from your trade for being so good at what you do. However, guilt may set in, because as a winner you see that it was the team who contributed and whose efforts should actually be acknowledged, not just your own. For example, have you ever heard an Oscar winner say, 'Well actually this award is not mine. It belongs to the make-up artist, the producer, the director and everyone who contributed towards making this film.' You can identify with that, and you may see this as fair and just since your relationship with your team is very important.

You are very creative and sometimes your demands on yourself for perfection may mean that you feel emotional at work, and look to your workmates to support you when a project or idea doesn't work out quite the way you planned. At these times you may appreciate a hug or a kiss from your colleagues to reassure you, and a relaxed working environment can be conducive to your happiness and to your work output. Sometimes you get so stuck into your work that you get carried away and don't even stop to eat or notice that the clock has long passed going-home time. Perhaps you get so involved with a project or with a piece of work because you are doing it over and over again in order to try to gain perfection, or because you have somehow got lost in doing the job. And at other times you may take a long time doing your work and labour over it because you want to do it properly and without having any pressure put upon you. Or you may meander on with your work because there are too many other distractions.

You may be a famous fashion designer, musician, artist, doctor or nurse, but having the support of a team is what really counts.

LOVERS

With a 7 influencing your love life then one of the key issues in your relationships is to break through the illusion of living in fantasy about your lover, and to come out of your dream world, and into reality. You have a terrific imagination and are prone to invent all sorts of scenarios in your head which simply don't exist, or if they do exist on the scale of one to ten they probably rate very low. A whole different life goes on all by itself in your mind and you can be prone to confusing fact with fiction. For example, your new lover takes you out on a date, and you may look into what they say and give it more meaning than its literal translation. 'I'd like to live in a house with a red rug,' pipes your lover, and you translate it into, 'He knows I have a red rug at my home and he wants to come and live with me.' On occasion your lover may be hinting what you think, but exaggerating the truth about a situation is your forte and can cause you much grief and heartache. However, if you have worked on this issue within your relationships then you tend to look at the facts before presuming things about your lover's meanings.

With a 7, you may find yourself attracted to lovers who are larger than life, who promise you the moon, or who are famous or whom you feel stand out from the crowd. This really allows your imagination to run wild and to imagine all sorts of unusual scenarios. Sometimes making up stories and having a dream to follow can help you to cope with everyday living in the real world. For example, if someone close to you dies then having a pipe dream and a lover who really takes you out of yourself and out of this world can help you to survive the dark times. Of course, eventually the stark reality of life brings you back down to earth – often with a bump.

Your lover may also be attracted to you because of your vivid imagination which improves life for him or her too, particularly in your sex life together. You have the ability to create illusions about yourself on a grand scale, and may tell 'porky pies' about who you are to guarantee your lover's attentions and to encourage him or her to like you or to stay around. But you are the one who can lose out here: in the end if your performance in bed or your qualifications don't match your descriptions then they may lose interest if they feel like they are dealing with a fake or someone who isn't being real. This can teach you to get real fast, or you may move on to the next lover to string along into your dream world too.

With a 7 you may prefer to find a lover whom you can love at a distance, for example, somebody who lives in another part of town or who has their own life to live without you playing too much of a part in it, so you only see them from time to time. Perhaps sharing closeness with a lover only occasionally is as much reality as you can take at times. With a 7 you are by nature a loner and someone who likes to spend time in your own company, doing what you want and when you want – you can be self-centred. So with a part-time lover you are able to find all the space you need within your relationship.

Another method of trying to avoid the reality of being in relationship with your lover is by escaping to your spirituality, or spending more time reading books about philosophy and life than, for example, indulging in primal pleasures. Of course, your lover may share these interests too and perhaps you both are happy to go off on a journey of introspection and personal development work together. Perhaps your lover finds your deep philosophical interests attractive and is turned on by your spirituality and your mind, and feels you can teach him or her about the deeper aspects of life.

With the 7 influence you are incredibly sensitive, so much so that sometimes you feel as delicate as a new-born butterfly, and so vulnerable that you feel as transparent as its whispery wings. To cover this up you may project an air of hardness by pretending you don't care when your lover says things which hurt you; you do this to protect yourself by avoiding your feelings of emotional pain. Indeed, you can come across as uncaring and unloving but it is simply to mask your deep feelings which in matters of love really touch the inner you. Your hypersensitivity to life can also cause arguments with your lover as you tend to take things personally and to heart and are easily hurt. You can be cold and calculating when you want and venomous with your verbal attacks. However, your sensitivity is also a gift as you can really feel what is going on and react accordingly. You can be very gentle with your lover during times of sensitivity.

You may have many dreams but once you have set your sights on the lover of your dreams you will set your strong and positive mind on delivering him or her, très vite! Indeed you tend to follow your intuition about which lover to materialize into your life, but you can spend much time pondering your choice mentally before making a move. You have a strong intuition which annoys you when you ignore it and it turns out your guidance was correct, like attracting a lover who turns out to be not quite what you expect. With a 7 you have very high expectations and sometimes this means that you go for a long time without the comforts of a lover by your side. 'Why bother if they are not perfect?' you may think as time flies by and potential lovers fall by the wayside. You have a naivity about you and when you think you have found a perfect lover you may try to destroy that relationship when you eventually catch a glimpse of reality.

Sometimes you feel tortured by your naivety and disappointed that you failed to see through yet another lover who has let you down, and you may even torture yourself for being so stupid or naive. You may be very hard on yourself indeed, and 'beat yourself up' for being wrong about him or her. But that's life with the 7, until you learn to trust yourself and to trust that the lovers you attract to you are all part of the process of learning about love and life. Sometimes your vulnerability and openness and your willingness to give yourself two hundred per cent to your lover can mean that they feel open to take advantage of you or to use you, because you are much too open and naive. Or perhaps your lovers feel more protective towards you at times. However, letting life in, trusting life, experiencing life just as it is, can eventually lead you to enjoy living in the real world and facing physical reality.

With a 7 you may prefer lovers of either sex, as you are

nature-loving and you may like to see nature mirrored back in all its possible human aspects of sexuality. Perhaps you date both sexes at once to fully appreciate the nature inside you, or attract one lover at a time to explore your sexuality deeply. Perhaps you turn to the same sex (if you were heterosexual) or to the opposite sex (if you were homosexual or lesbian) because you have been wounded deeply by a lover of your regular preference in sex. However, sex may not play a large part in your relationship at all as exploring your sexuality has deeper issues which can be infinitely more important than the purely physical ones. With a 7 you can also be sexist and feel stuck in the role you play being one of either sex, perhaps in what you wear or by your attitudes towards your lover and life. However, nature learns to balance itself out by accepting all possibilities, including sexuality.

SEDUCTION, SEX AND AFFAIRS

With a 7 you may seduce a potential lover by making yourself totally and utterly theirs, like exposing yourself to them to make them feel welcome. Perhaps you may act all naive in order to get your potential lover to rescue and protect you as they whisk you off to a place of rest and play. You can be very provocative, and sometimes give the come-on by saying things naively without intending to seduce one lover when it was his or her friend who interested you. And you may wonder why when you are sitting in a micro skirt or other revealing clothes many lovers suddenly make themselves available to you. You can be blunt in your seduction techniques and like a black and white immediate response as you are impatient. An instant 'yes, now,' can be a real turn-on for you.

Sometimes you have an affair to explore another aspect of your sexuality, or because your primary partner hasn't lived up to your expectations in your relationship, and you seek satisfaction of these expectations elsewhere. Perhaps your sex life with your lover and your spiritual connection to your partner means that both these needs are fulfilled. You may naively tell your partner about your lover, and in a self-centred way think he or she will understand. An affair may help you with your personal development as you may focus on your internal world, or it may help you break down your illusions about life.

With a 7 influencing your sex life you can be very choosy and your expectations are often so high that celibacy seems a better option; perhaps you simply enjoy feeling sexual energy rather than doing something with it. However, like nature you like to fuse with everything and sex magic with your ideal lover is one distinct possibility. Sex is one of the exhilirating ways which helps you to feel real and to feel connected to your lover and to life. However, your sense of isolation at times means that when you are making love, your lover may see your detachment as rejection or that you are uninterested in him or her sexually. A shower before sex is often a prerequisite with the influence of a 7, and with your lover too – it can get very steamy. Sometimes you may like to feel physical pain in sex, and be turned on by a rough partner, particularly in foreplay. However, paradoxically pain and getting hurt by your lover may also be your biggest fear. Your aphrodisiac is appreciation, and you may fantasize about group sex with strangers you've just met.

FRIENDS

With a 7 influencing your friendships you often like to find a few close friends to relate to rather than going around with one large group of friends. This may be because you feel much safer with small numbers where you feel like you can connect with them. Within a large group you may lose your sense of identity and feel isolated because you feel left out and can't connect with everyone at once. Of course, you are by nature detached. But when you do feel this detachment within a group of friends and acquaintances you may then feel like they are leaving you out. Of course they may not be actually leaving you out of the group or its activities, but you may feel this because you are hypersensitive and can easily take offence.

With a 7 you may get despondent or gloomy at times when you feel you don't fit in or belong with any of your friends. You may even have an inferiority complex in certain situations or at different times in your life about yourself. However, as soon as you feel connected to one of your friends again it helps to restore your confidence in yourself and brings you back to life. You have a strong and positive mind and you like to give yourself a positive talking to, particularly at times when you feel like you are losing a grip on reality with yourself.

When you let friends get close to you it's usually because you have a strong connection, particularly a spiritual connection to them. Perhaps you meditate with them, or do yoga, or go on spiritual retreats. Usually you are very fussy about who you let into your home and your life, and into your sacred space. However you can be naive and when forming new friendships open your door too wide and let all and sundry in. You like to share your feelings with your friends but if they betray those confidences you can be very nasty indeed, or turn it in on yourself and introspect, and avoid facing or dealing with reality.

Sometimes you can be too introspective and dreamy, and even though you may be having a good time drifting around in your imagination, your friends like to see you, and may persuade you to go out with them and socialize. A bit of fun and noise can soon bring you around to physical reality. With a 7 you sometimes rely on your friends too much and take them for granted when they do so much for you. They rarely seem to match your high expectations, because being self-centred you expect their lives to constantly revolve around you twenty-four hours a day.

With the 7, your friends may find you too picky. When you are arranging to go to a restaurant you may say, 'That one's too cold, that one's too noisy, too expensive . . .' and so on. Sometimes you get too bogged down with physical reality. This can make you appear difficult to your friends at times, and spoil their fun and relaxation. Even though you are truly very sensitive to your environment sometimes you need to toughen up. Your friends will not always put up with your demands and you may eventually learn the art of compromise. However, you can be polite and courteous when you want to be and when you think of your friends' needs instead of only your own. With a 7 you can indeed make a brilliant host or hostess with your gift for bringing people together and arranging a perfect night out.

FAMILY

With a 7 in your chart you may have been brought up by parents who encouraged your creativity and imagination and allowed you to fantasize freely about life by having larger-than-life dreams which you were not always able to materialize. For example, if you fantasized about being the world's number one ballet dancer, sure it was possible, but did they encourage you to take ballet class? However, as an adult you often have the habit of getting what you want, when you really, really want it, and therefore you know that you can materialize your dreams yourself. And you are wonderful at making your family's dreams come true too.

You may not see your parents or other siblings very often because you tend to isolate yourself and live in your own little world. You like to have the space to contemplate your navel when and where you wish. Perhaps they think you don't need them because you seem so detached and self reliant, and you can manage nicely by yourself. You dislike your extended family interfering or edging their way into your and your partner's or children's lives. You like to be able to choose when and where you see them on your terms because you can be self-centred. With a 7 you are very protective towards them, however, and when there are family troubles you are good at rallying support from each other and bringing the family together.

You need space within your relationship with your partner. Even if it is only ten minutes a day, then this gives you time to think, and to replenish your energies by reconnecting with your inner self. Sometimes you may opt to do the gardening, or any solitary chore, in order to gain some time by yourself if there are a lot of people in your

123

family. Or you may even get sick (like a headache!) if you don't get some time on your own, or even invent some hypochondriac complaint to give you some space. You may need to be aware that because you have such a powerful mind, if you think too much that you need space you may create your partner going away for longer periods than you would so desire. Since your partner is close to you they will usually pick up when you need to be left alone.

Family life may be challenging to you because you can feel isolated and feel like you are an outsider in the family, and that you don't belong to the group. Particularly when you feel that some family member doesn't respect you, you are very sensitive and you may stay away from them, even if a part of this isn't reality and is locked up in your imagination. You may reject your family to protect yourself from getting hurt by them rejecting you. And sometimes your fear of rejection makes you open to putting yourself on the outside and feeling isolated from the group. However, you can be naive and gullible sometimes and as a result of your sensitivity your partner, parents, and even your children, may make you feel like the scapegoat of the family.

With a 7 in your chart you can be a real role model for your family by showing them how to connect with others spiritually as well as providing them with their material needs. Your family can also help you by keeping you aware of their needs which helps to keep your feet on the ground, so that you don't get too lost within yourself and lose a grip on reality.

WORK RELATIONSHIPS

With a 7 in your chart you can be a bit of a loner and you may like to work for yourself, or alone, so that you can limit time spent with others, and because you are so sensitive. But if you do find yourself working for a large organization or with lots of people around then you may need your own office or corner space which you can call your own. Indeed you may manage to converse with your workmates during work hours but during lunchtimes or breaks you may be found sitting on your own in the staff restaurant or sitting alone in a quiet place contemplating, or reading a book. Hence, a job as a researcher where your head is buried deeply in your work may be perfect for you, as you fail to notice anybody else exists. And even if you are a city trader the high level of concentration constantly needed means that although you are surrounded by other traders they and you are living in your own separate worlds.

With a 7 in your chart you are highly motivated and you like to instigate things and bring your projects and work to fruition.

Sometimes lapsing into daydreaming while you are working on an important project or losing your grip on reality when you are just about to clinch a deal could be extremely fatal. You are prone to panic when things go right as much as when they go wrong, particularly because you lose your 'centredness' about where you are and get fearful of what might happen. For example, you may panic about your promotion to managing director at work because although you are very successful you haven't played that role before and your vivid imagination throws up all kinds of fears. Success also brings you more into the real world because it generally gives you more practical responsibilities. However, you have the ability to turn to your workmates for support even when you are managing director, and you like to think that they will help you with your work if you need.

People at work are often inspired by your energy and your ability to get through work so quickly, and you may be multi-talented. Indeed you are a fast learner and you pick up all the tricks of the trade in no time at all, and are often pernickety about detail. All the t's will be crossed and the i's dotted with you. With the influence of the 7 you are able to encourage your workmates to work hard and do better and you are able to motivate them, perhaps by being a role model to them, and perhaps by showing them how to use creative visualization to help them too. You may be tempted to bring your spirituality into the work place and perhaps organize a meditation or relaxation group for your colleagues (something which you may well like doing in groups too).

With a 7 you can be a perfectionist and you may wind your workmates up by insisting that they do things your way, or by taking on more of their work because you think you can make a perfect and better job out of it than them. You may also wind them up with your comments about life, and you may deliberately provoke them to get them to react at times. With a 7 you may also react negatively to them or to their constructive criticism or even to the slightest thing your workmates say – you are hypersensitive. You may evade them when they try to get you to work in a way which suits them, which would help you in your job, because you are self-centred and like to do things your way. You take criticism personally and it may take you quite a while to trust your boss, for example, if he took you to task over your work, even if it was for the best.

LOVERS

With the 8 in your chart you ooze charm and charisma and with the sweep of your strong energy towards your lover, he or she simply falls at your feet. You could charm the wings off a butterfly without it noticing, and you can charm your lover into doing things they wouldn't even think possible – either in or out of the bedroom. You may say that this means you have the ability to pull the wool over your lover's eyes, but indeed they do things with their eyes fully open and focused on you! You do not have to turn on this charm when you find yourself in urgent need of it because it is always there at your fingertips – it is in your whole being. It is likely your lover loves to do things for you because they feel charmed and lucky to be with you. Have all these compliments gone to your head? Well, you can understand then why with an 8 you can also be extremely big-headed, conceited and full of your own momentous self-importance – but that can also be a turn-on for some lovers too.

You may choose a lover who mirrors your pedigree, someone who is happy to go around looking in the mirror all day, with a streak of vanity which leaves Casanova behind by a milestone. Or whom you can swan around the world with arm in arm being beautiful, rich, successful and, hopefully, be some of the happiest lovers too. However, when it comes to romance you can be insecure, because with such a big ego to live up to, it can let you down if you get hurt by a lover who walks all over you. Perhaps this is your karma because you can manipulate your lover and walk all over him or her too. But you do have a conscience, and you may have learned that hurting a lover deliberately because they have scorned you may not always be the answer. And it may cause extra aggravation for you.

Sometimes, with an 8, you may like to hunt, or to be hunted, and you like the feel of the chase, particularly when you first meet your lover, but also later on, because being chased makes you feel secure knowing that you are wanted. And chasing gives you the control to say, 'I'm in charge and I want this lover with me.' Of course, you don't always get what you want, you get what you need. Some lovers may not like to be chased, and you may not like it either. Sometimes you go through stages of being passive then assertive with your lover, and this can be all in the space of a day, so your lover may need to be adaptable to you. This behaviour can lead to power struggles if you both try to assume control at the same time. Or if you are both passive at similar times then you can experience a gentleness and an altogether different feel to your relationship.

With the influence of the 8, of course, you may like your lover to take control of you (and if you are very wilful they may need to!) by organizing your time together, and you may be happy to submit. Particularly if in other areas of your life you are always needing to be in charge then time out with your lover may be essential. You are also happy for your lover to pay for you when you go out for a meal, and so on, but you may like to think that you can equally provide. For example, you may offer to pay for dinner, but be happy when your lover pays for you instead. Money can be an issue with your lover, particularly if they spend your money like water and you let them take control of you!

In relationship with your lover you may find a challenge in letting go of control and having fun, partially because you are a rather responsible person and you have a seriously successful reputation to live up to. And also because you may at times be lacking in humour and like to remain an adult, and adults don't fall about laughing if they are being terribly responsible. Of course, if you take life that seriously (and yourself too) then no matter how beautiful, rich or successful you are, your lover is going to get bored with you if you can't share a joke with them. Indeed you may seem quite heavy-going at times and finding a lover with a sense of the ridiculous may be essential. Laughing is really good for you and learning to relax with your lover may even help to improve your quality of life.

You may be serious but once you have learned to relax then your underlying feelings of insecurity vanish to some degree and the lovely, romantic person lingering just under the skin is allowed to surface. Of course, you may need some lessons from your lover to show you the ropes but you steadily catch on. With an 8 you love flattery, and a little encouragement when you have been extra romantic towards your lover can boost your confidence and head you in the right direction. You can be flattering too, and you may find it easier to flatter your lover with gifts and flowers than to say 'I love you' or to read out romantic poetry which isn't really your scene. Whatever, relaxation is the key and exercise and sex can really help to loosen you up.

With an 8 in your chart you may have developed the skill of strength in your life, particularly through some of the tough experiences which may have come your way. Life may have dealt you an Ace, or a One in numerological terms, and with both of these numbers strength is what has helped you to face all the situations in your life and with your lovers. You may like and need a lover who is a pillar of strength to you because you are tired of being strong, or your lover may be equally strong so that you just need to take care of yourself. A lover who is feeble and weak, or who has no confidence in their appearance (although you may be able to see his or her beauty), may also attract you, so that you can share your strength with them and make them strong (again) too. You love to empower people, and to see them grow in a positive way. And even if your lover leaves you after you have helped in their process of finding their own strength, then you are genuinely pleased that they are in some way a happier person.

You are a powerful and forceful person at times and your lover may feel overpowered by your insistence about what you should do together, where you should go together, when you should do it, or even what they should wear in your company. You may come up against a brick wall if you carry on like this all the time and with all these shoulds there is no room for spontaneity or relaxation. However, you have a gentle side to your nature and learning to relax about your itinerary and life together may prolong the relationship and help to keep yours and his or her sanity too.

With the 8 in your chart you may not take to being manipulated or to a lover who shows signs of possessiveness over you. Nobody owns you and even when you have given your heart to your lover, your soul is not for sale and is not negotiable. You may get very angry and aggressive indeed (and even violent) if you feel possessed or pursued by a lover from whom you feel you can't escape. However, this is in the extreme, and usually if you do find yourself in this situation it is because you have strong karmic links or ties to your lover from the past or from a past life. For example, if your lover bought you as a slave in a past life and in this life they tried to possess you, well then, yes, you may get very angry indeed towards them. Or you may try to own or possess them by trying to manipulate and control their life too. In karmic relationships, what you give out, you get back.

SEDUCTION, SEX AND AFFAIRS

Power can turn you on, and if your potential lover offers you the chance of a ride on his or her multi-engined, high-powered designer motorbike, where you can feel its power throbbing between your thighs, then you may be easily persuaded. Of course that is not the only thing you like between your legs but it makes good foreplay. With an 8 if you are so charming then you probably get offers all the time, and if you are fed up of the overt chat-up lines, then subtlety may be a big turn-on. So a potential lover who keeps you guessing and gets you to do all the work may appeal to you. You can also appear to others as a sex object and a potential lover who sees behind your charm, perhaps Joe or Joanne Bloggs with a kind heart, can send your pulse racing because you realize sex isn't the only thing on his or her mind on your first date and you feel they really want to know *you*.

One of the reasons you may start an affair is because you are feeling controlled by your partner in your primary relationship, and you seek to take control of your life by doing something out of their control. Sometimes you can find love with your lover if your partner is uncaring and very preoccupied with materialism. Or perhaps you have a spiritual connection with your lover which helps to take you away from the material pressures within your primary relationship. Failure with your partner or your lover can help you to do some soul-searching and take you inside of yourself.

With an 8 in your chart then sex is one of your favourite subjects and although your aphrodisiac is often money, sex comes a close runner-up, with or without foreplay. Sex is one way for you to show to your lover who's in control and daytime power games are often taken into the bedroom. Having the biggest bulges may be your idea of attraction, but even if size doesn't shape up to your usual require-ments then what you wear does. Slit skirts, sexy suits, tight-fitting clothes which offer resistance when they are taken off can add to the suspense, and red or black under-wear can all heighten your desires and anticipation. You may also put a lot of pressure on yourself about your performance and may not be so bothered about pleasing your lover as much as convincing your ego that you are ace. You may like to play control games like tying each other up by the hands, using sex toys such as dildos, and you may fantasize about master and slave domination. Being out of control and dominated may also be one of your biggest fears.

FRIENDS

With the 8 in your chart then you may feel sure of yourself and be someone who likes to lead your own life, and to stand on your own two feet. Your friends may be attracted to you because you appear to be so powerful, or because you project an air of coolness and control and it seems to them like you have it all. Perhaps you are very rich, or very beautiful, or have a lot of external power and responsibilities, and your friends think this will rub off on them too.

However, unless you think that your friends are of equal standing to you then you are unlikely to give them the time of day. Perhaps it is out of your inner insecurity or fear of failure which you may see in them (even if they are happy with their lives). Of course, when you have such a lot according to your standards you may fear losing everything: losing your looks, losing your charm, your money or your power, or losing your powerful friends too. Perhaps you treat your friends like material possessions, or see them only at your convenience, or perhaps you try to buy their friendships by lavishing money and possessions on them. Then you can feel like they owe you something, or that you hold some sort of control over their lives. However, people don't like to be manipulated and at some point your super cool will become super fool, as your 'friends' quietly exit by slipping out the back door and out of your life, possibly for good.

With an 8 you may think you don't need anybody, right, and your friends just get in your way. Wrong! Your friends can help you to keep the balance in your life, because with so much emphasis on success you need to be able to go out and party and forget about your self-importance. Friends can also help you to develop your spiritual connection with yourself and with the rest of life so that you are not separated on an island by yourself. Finding the inner you can give you strength and make success even more rewarding, and you can then share your success with your friends to empower their lives too.

When you have learned to respect yourself then you may see all your friends as equal and treat them with respect too, no matter who they are or what they do. There is every reason with your bright intellectual mind and your spark of charisma that you can magnetically draw many friends into your life. Indeed from sporting events, to scintillating private dinner parties, to celebrity bashes, you share an active social life. With an 8 you are also as likely to go on a spiritual retreat or go riding in the countryside with your friends away from the pressures of society, as attending a grand gala.

You can remain a bit of a mystery to your friends because sometimes you are assertive and busy organizing your group events, and at other times you're so passive that you barely get around to telephoning them. However, they probably enjoy both extremes and everything in between about you with the influence of the 8, and are aware of these patterns of behaviour. For you, at times when you want to be quiet and gentle you probably do pick up the telephone but to call people who share this

135

same quality as you, and you may do the same when you are feeling very active too.

FAMILY

With an 8 in your chart you are very stubborn; perhaps because you were brought up in a family of headstrong people where there was a battle of wills going on, or because you had to be stubborn to win any battles at all. Perhaps you threw tantrums when you didn't get your own way as a child, and perhaps you still do. You may have also bullied other children in your family or been quietly manipulative so that you got your own way without resorting to aggression or violence. You may still start more than your fair share of family fights and failure is not an option – you like to win.

You are a very responsible person and as you learn to balance your passive side with your active, assertive side then you may turn to working on win/win situations between yourself and your family members, and finding the middle ground. And if your family do find themselves in a position of failure financially you may well quickly jump in to rescue them if you can, knowing that your reward is their success and that they will pay you back when they can. With an 8 you know how to stand on your own two feet but sometimes you may seek advice from your family about your material and financial responsibilities, to make sure that they are all in order and looked after properly.

With the influence of the 8 you like to be proud of your family and to take pride in their achievements, and in how wonderful they are even if they don't hold any trophies to their name. Your partner or children will be on the top of that list, as well as all your extended family. You like flattery too, and when you have successes in your life you may expect your whole family to celebrate and to make a big fuss of you.

When you are choosing a partner, particularly one whom you think is destined to become part of your family, you may look for someone whom you know is responsible and can look after themselves (and your children). You may be a cosmopolitan person who looks for a perfect partner from another country or for someone with a completely different background. With an 8 in your chart you can be insecure and particularly when you first go out with a new partner you may constantly test and try them to see if they are keen. Sometimes your pushing and pulling at the same time tests them too much and they walk away seemingly exhausted with the games which you play. However, you test because you feel insecure and once you feel safe within yourself and with your new partner you may get really serious about them and stop fooling around. Choosing a partner is a serious issue to you anyway.

With the 8 in your chart you may let your family take control of you by giving away your power to them. For example, by letting them have a very large say about how you run your life even when you are married or have a regular partner. Sometimes they may also encourage you to have self-control when your life gets out of hand, instead of your family holding your hand. However, by stepping into your own power, making your own decisions and relying on your own backbone to support you, then you can feel in control of your own destiny again. With your own inner strength you can then make a success out of your own life, instead of relying on your family's strength and success to provide.

WORK RELATIONSHIPS

You are a smart Alec and you are shrewd, and this can help you in the field of business (particularly big business) as you know all about wheeling and dealing. You have real business flair and a head for finances and you know how to look after yourself in any company. You may measure success by how much you earn, the big car you drive and so on, but success to you may also mean putting through a deal which is worthwhile for both sides in an agreement.

With an 8, being successful at your job makes you a popular employee and a good business colleague as you bring success to their lives too. Your work commitments may take priority over your friendships at work and although your charm and magnetism mean you have plenty of choice for company, work often comes first. However, you are not averse to socializing with your workmates if it's work your talking about, and you may also take the opportunity to boast about your achievements or to butter up potential clients who are socializing with you. You know how to cajole when there is something you want.

Sex is also one of your favourite subjects to talk about even at work, and when work gets too pressurized out come the jokes or out comes some serious discussion with your workmates over lunch. With the influence of the 8 you have the ability to work hard and play hard too.

With an 8 in your chart you like money, status and recognition for a job well done, and you like being a leader and in control. Sometimes your work colleagues may find you an indomitable force, particularly when you want to work on your terms or not at all, which can mean that you are pretty rigid in your outlook, and even tyrannical at times. You like to be the boss and to have some authority in your job, and you may enjoy competing with your workmates, except when it leads to a clashing and dashing of egos. Indeed, you are willing to fight for what you want and if it's promotion you are after then you may distance yourself from your closest work colleagues – who are in direct competition with you – in order to go for what you want.

Sometimes it may be that you are too scared of taking your own power, and therefore turn down the reward of promotion at work in order to keep yourself in a smaller role because you are scared of being powerful or taking on extra responsibilities. With the influence of the 8 you have a gentle and caring side to your nature, and you can be quite spiritual. You may take success and recognition at work in your stride, and share it quietly with your closest work colleagues, or with a few close friends or family.

With an 8 you are conscientious and rock steady at work, and you like to dress smart or look sexy, and your power and strength really shine through with confidence; you are in control of you. At times you can be ostentatious and show off, but generally your work colleagues like you for your directness because you seem to feel comfortable simply being who you are. You don't try to cover up your faults, you wave them around and you may even be proud of them at times. Indeed you can be a real guide at work and help to organize a better life for others.

LOVERS

With the 9 in your chart then you are a pleaser, and a pleaser who says, 'Please, please me too' – you like it both ways. However, you have an enormous capacity to give to your lover and your reward is simply seeing your lover happy and content. This is because you have a streak of selflessness within you and can go on giving and giving, which to others may seem like a one-way street. What they don't realize is that you get so much pleasure from giving that you receive naturally. Of course, you may attract a lover who appreciates you giving to him or her and who lavishes you with love and attention. You can be self-indulgent and lavish yourself with pleasure too, but it feels even nicer when you are lavished with attention by your lover!

You know how to give and sometimes when you are being very selfish you think that 'this is not OK' because you were born to give. Of course, getting selfish from time to time may be necessary. For example, if your lover appears to be taking advantage of your giving nature, it may be essential for you to be selfish to show to him or her you have feelings and are entitled to some returns too. Your lover may be shocked to find out that he or she needs to learn to give to you (perhaps you are teaching them this by being in relationship with them), and that they need to make an effort too. However, you may find it difficult to be selfish for too long at a time.

With a 9 in your chart you are one of life's liberated lovers and you may attract to you a lover who feels free to express him or herself and whom is adaptable in and out of the bedroom. You may like to go out with your lover to an art gallery, to a musical concert, to visit an historical sight or go to the trendiest high-flying party in town. You like to experience all walks of life and to fit in with whomever is around. Indeed, your coat has many colours and it is constantly changing. Sometimes when you are out with different types of people your lover may be surprised when you reveal aspects of yourself which are completely new to him or her. This can be very exciting for your lover because even if you have been living together or dating for a long time, there are still lots of interesting surprises with you.

However, you may take on different identities when you are around different people, and you can accommodate different kinds of lovers, but sometimes you do this to fall in line with them in order to avoid rocking the boat and because you want them to like you. Although you are a master of disguises you can get lost in being whom your lover wants you to be rather than stamping your own identity into the relationship whether they like it or not and saying, 'This is me.' You are a pleaser and you may think that by going along with your lover's needs then you will make them happy so that they will like you even more, and want to keep you in their lives.

With the 9 in your chart you can be very artistic,

creative, and musical and you can be very emotional too. Your lover may be called upon to be flexible with you when you are in one of your black moods. Indeed, you have a fiery temper which seems to emerge out of nowhere, and goes just as soon. But your sensitivity means that you feel things deeply and experience the fire and the passion of life within you – your lover can reap the rewards of this in your sex life together. Your fieriness can be wonderful in the bedroom. Perhaps your lover shares your passion for creativity and you paint together, or have a party where you play the guitar while your lover plays the drums or other musical instruments to entertain your friends, or dance the night away.

With a 9 you have very high expectations of your lover and when he or she doesn't match them then you can be critical of him or her and nag them too. But generally you have a laid-back and relaxed approach to life and if your lover criticizes you it may go right over your head, or you simply make some sarcastic remark to cut them dead. You are good enough at criticizing yourself without getting it from your lover too. You can be quite lazy at times and wander around the home in your most casual of clothes, and not make too much of an effort when your lover's around. If your lover does make demands for you to smarten up then you may do so for a while, but feel cheesed off that he or she doesn't accept you the way that you are. However, at the end of the day you like to feel loved and you may dress up to the nines, even if it annoys you, to please your lover and to feel accepted.

You are witty, satirical and you know how to entertain your lover with literary wizardry for more than an afternoon. With a 9 influencing your life you may find a lover who is brilliantly intelligent or intellectual, who can help to keep your mind stimulated too. Indeed you have a worldly view and your interest in humanitarian issues may be at the top of the list for discussion. So a lover with a head and a heart and a conscience may really attract you. You can be a perfectionist and want your partner to be a Jack of all trades even though he or she may be a master of none. For example, loving, good-looking and dishy, good in bed, passionate, creative, intelligent, and interested in politics and religion, and healthy and wealthy too. No wonder you criticize your lover when you find out he or she lives up to only two or three items on your list, which is constantly growing with more and more requisites.

With a 9 you are open to life and you like to sail along with the flow and take it as it comes. However, there is a side to you which can be conservative (perhaps from the way you were brought up), in which case you will put expectations onto yourself about being in relationship. For example, if you have been going out with your lover for a long time, then your conditioning from childhood may tell you that in order to move in with your lover you need to get married first. This traditional but narrow-minded outlook may be outdated and even though you may be liberated in many ways, this mindset may pester you and not go away. You may fear people judging you and find yourself in a moral dilemma if you decide to live together with your lover without tying the knot. However, with a 9 you also possess an incredibly rebellious attitude and you are strong-willed, and you will usually do what you want in the end without anyone else's blessing or moral consent. You may also swop one lover for the next as you find out about what suits you best, whether others approve of you or not! Experimenting is the game. Sometimes experimenting with different lovers means that you find yourself in situations which are uncomfortable, perhaps when you have fallen for the wrong type. Of course, there is no right or wrong, and every lover who finds themself on your path can improve your worldly general knowledge about relationships and teach you about life. However, if you find you are careless when you are being footloose and fancy free then being a little discriminating about the facts and thinking things through before you dive into a relationship can help make life easier for you. Of course with a 9 you may enjoy the idea of being in relationships with the 'wrong' type of lover and at every opportunity remind people around you that they are in your life simply to shock them. You can be highly mischievous and with your wonderful satirical sense of humour and relaxed attitudes you can encourage others to see the funny side of life.

SEDUCTION, SEX AND AFFAIRS

If you project the prudish or conservative side to the 9 energy then a potential lover needs to firstly make you laugh, and secondly get you a little tipsy to relax you, and thirdly simply offer to take you home to their place and give you a massage for your poor aching neck. It's easy, and as you like to please your lover then you will generally go along with his or her plans. If you are a liberated lover then you may come on all passionate and wanting from the first moment you set eyes on your luscious lover. And with all that steam and your promises of pleasure (which you are quite capable of delivering later on) how can they resist? However, a real Renaissance Man or Woman may turn you on by impressing you with their knowledge, and a potential lover may seduce you with their credentials of social standing or power.

You may start an affair with a lover because you face so much criticism or have such high demands and expectations placed upon you by your primary partner that you need to relieve all the pressure. And if your passion or creativity with your partner has been stifled then it will need to be expressed somewhere. An affair can teach you to accept your own imperfection, particularly if you are a moralist who likes to live by the book. You may openly experiment with lots of lovers and expect your partner to be understanding about them because you can be so utterly selfish.

With a 9 in your chart then you may see your sex life as one big experiment and you can be anything from soft and playful to really wild, and everything in between as you are so adaptable to your lovers, and you like to please. Perhaps your aphrodisiac is a lover in a uniform who disciplines you to be a good girl or boy sexually, or you and your lover join in wild parties or orgies where condoms are used liberally. You love deep kissing, and foreplay of nibbles and wine may take on a different perspective than its traditional meaning. Your motto may be 'I'm in service' and indeed you may fantasize about being a prostitute or courtesan. You like power and your sometimes perfectionist nature means that you may look for a lover who is the best in his or her field, so even if they are not powerful in bed they are powerful out of it. You may fear not being good enough and this may cause you some concern in your sex life even if it isn't a fact. Brains may be more important than brawn, and a strong spiritual connection with your lover can mean that you enjoy sex whatever you do.

FRIENDS

You are passionate about life and you like to get out and have fun with your friends at any available opportunity – you love to socialize. You can be loud and extrovert and sometimes like to take a trip on the wild side of life by visiting a strip joint with your friends for a fun night out (nothing seems to shock you). And at other times you may be quiet and demure as you discuss current affairs or your spirituality with your friends. You can get along with most people and your openness, friendliness and your adaptability makes you very popular and in demand socially.

With a 9 in your chart, sometimes you can be highly opinionated and feel superior to your friends by thinking you know more than they do. Of course, you always like to be right and once you are on your high horse about a topic then it takes a good knock to get you down. You may love it when your friends challenge your opinions and you like it even more when you win them over to your opinion or on to your side. This makes you feel powerful, but your arguments can seem pretty petty at times. However, at least you do have something to say for yourself, and you are forging your own strong identity instead of going with the consensus of your friends' opinions and falling in line with them to seek their approval. And it makes you interesting to them.

With the influence of the 9 you tend to follow your own beliefs and you may live your life by peppering your

147

conversations with shoulds all the time. For example, by saying to your friend, 'I believe you should work harder at your job, or, 'You should get rid of that jumper, it doesn't suit you'! Sometimes you can be sanctimonious and behave like a 'holy cow' and while it's your choice to feel that you are better than your friends, they don't need to compare their lives with you, or live up to your expectations. Indeed, at times you can ram your opinions down your friends' throats by letting them know in no uncertain terms how they should live their lives. You may well find a decrease in your popularity stakes at these times.

You are a loving and caring person and it is in your giving nature to help your friends and do things for them whenever they need. However, sometimes you can give too much and end up with no time or energy left for yourself. For example, you lead a hectic lifestyle, but you are always willing to drop everything for your friends to help them out, day or night. Of course you get such pleasure from giving, but sometimes you need to get selfish and say 'not now' in order for you to maintain your healthy survival. You can't give if you have collapsed with exhaustion so stop and think, and do what is fair for all concerned within the situation – then you can please everybody.

Mystical topics may appeal to you, and you may feel a strong psychic connection to some of your friends. Perhaps you dream about them or get premonitions about what may be in store, and they are often along the right lines. You may also like to share some of your psychic experiences with your friends, particularly if they are psychic too. However, with a 9, you can use your strong discriminating mind to keep a check on your psychic feel-ings, to help you keep a grip on reality.

FAMILY

With the 9 in your chart you may have been brought up to be a good girl or boy who was told to be on your best behaviour, particularly when there were family around. Not that you always were, mind, and you may have been punished for stepping out of line and being rebellious at times. Punishment may have been humiliating, particularly if when you were naughty your parents punished you in front of the family, or told them how naughty you had been in front of you, or perhaps you felt humiliated by being sent to your room. However, crime meant punish-ment so when you knew you had done something wrong you may have tried to cover it up (and maybe you still do).

However, you have a real sense of what it is like to be approved or disapproved of and you can be like this towards your family. For example, if you and your partner are both invited to a family event then you may be disap-proving of your partner going without your permission. Sometimes you also need to allow yourself permission to act in a certain way or to do things for yourself. For example, if you really need a break from your partner (and your children) you may feel selfish by wanting to go on a holiday by yourself, and even when they are happy for you to go, you need to give your own permission. With a 9 at times you do the appropriate thing instead of what your gut instincts are telling you, or vice versa, and this can lead to conflicts within yourself and with your family.

You may require your partner and children to live up to

your high expectations and think it's just not good enough when they don't conform. For example, when your partner irons your shirts or skirts you like them to be pristine and folded precisely in the right way. Sometimes you can be really hard on them but underneath you have a caring and sensitive side which means you really try to understand they are not perfect, and neither are you for being so impossible at times. Letting go and relaxing by bringing some of the carefree energy of the 9 into your life can help you to let go of expectations and lead a happier life.

Family values are really important to you and you may judge your family by their values too; if your brother doesn't behave in the way he should towards your family then you can get very critical indeed. Your partner may also need to share similar values to you, and if they are more broad-minded than you it can cause friction in the relationship, and also help you to see life in a different way. Of course, you may be searching for the ideal partner, perhaps one with the same background, the same religion, or who has been educated at the same school; intelligence is important to you. Education is important too, and with your humanitarian interests then a concern for the welfare of others (not just themselves) may also be a prerequisite.

With the 9 teaching comes naturally to you, and your family are often inspired by your sense of values, your moral codes, and also by your altruistic attitude in loving and giving to your family selflessly. You lead by your fine example, and take into consideration your gut instincts about what is best for you and your family in life, rather than trying desperately to be seen to be politically correct and always doing the right thing.

WORK RELATIONSHIP

You are a born leader and even if you do not like using this talent or gift you are often called upon to do so, and usually, as you like to please people, you will follow it through. Using your leadership skills can help you to find direction in your life and help everyone you work with too. With a 9 influencing your work life you may also lead by example, and your work colleagues can be very impressed and inspired by your skills. However, when it comes to socializing (which usually plays a large part in your working life) then you may feel equal to your work-mates even if you are their boss, and you may insist on first-name terms. Indeed, you love a pint and a gossip as much as they do and you would not like to feel left out because of your job title.

Sometimes you like to command approval from your colleagues at work and you may do this by seemingly being one of the crowd and agreeing with their opinions about, say, how to handle a work project, when you really don't. You know when to keep your mouth shut so that you feel accepted by your workmates. However, you also know how to show others up when they have overstepped their mark by disagreeing with your almighty opinions at times, whether they like you for it or not. But it is usually because you truly believe in your methods about how to get the work done, which can improve life for them and everyone – you don't do it just to benefit yourself.

With the 9 in your chart you like fairness at work, fair trade, fair behaviour, fair pay, and you are willing to stand up for you and your workers' rights. You believe in equality and like to see everyone treated in the same way, so that there are not one set of rules for some and another set for others. You use your strong opinions to make sure that your voice is heard, and that their voice gets heard too. However, if you think the system isn't treating you in a fair way at work then you are likely to design your own set of rules to work by, and your rebellious nature can certainly get you noticed in a big way. Even when you work quietly you can be a bit of a revolutionary in your own way.

With a 9 in your chart you can be religious and you may insist on wearing your religion on your sleeve, and think that everyone at work should agree with your religious beliefs. Indeed, they may respect you greatly for being true to yourself and for following the set of rules laid out by your religion. However, it is up to you to respect your workmates by accepting them the way they are too, so that you can all appreciate each other's uniqueness (whatever their background or religion). The knowledge from all religions is expansive and learning a little about different religions can only enrich your life and widen your love for each other and humanity.

At times you can be easy-going and so open and friendly that everyone feels comfortable in your presence, but you can be so relaxed that you end up talking to everyone and not getting much work done. Learning about the human heart and soul is important to you, so you may choose a career which allows you lots of human contact so that you can serve them and fulfil your needs too. With a 9, the more you give to people the happier you become and the more work (you all) get done.

PART THREE

YOUR RELATIONSHIP
COMPARISON
NUMBERS

6

Working Out Your
Comparison Numbers

ONCE you know how to work out your own numerology chart (see pages 30–37, Chapter 4), then you can go on to learn how to compare your chart with somebody else's. It doesn't matter if you are comparing yourself and your sister, or lover, or a member of your staff, or your children, because with all your relationships the method remains the same. That is, you simply add your numbers together to get a final digit which you can then look up in the following chapter to find out highlights of your potential, your strengths and challenges together.

You can find out about all different aspects of your life together. For example, if you are working or living with someone and you would like to find out highlights of your potential on the nitty-gritty, day-to-day basis, then you would refer to your Personality Numbers, by simply adding these together. Your Life Purpose Numbers together highlight your soul connection and the larger goal or picture you are working on together. Your Karma or Wisdom Numbers added up highlight past (life) issues together, and practical qualities you may be working with as a result in this lifetime – your karmic interactions.

Your first names together highlight a major focus or goal together – your Goal Numbers. And finally your Personal Year Numbers together indicate what experiences may be highlighted during a specific year.

Remember when adding up your Personal Year Numbers that each time one of you has a birthday this number will change, and alter the issues or experiences which you may both be working on together in your relationship, during that time. Therefore, your comparison Personal Year Number may not last a full year unless your birthdays fall on the same date as each other.

When you are looking up your joint numbers for yourself and family, friends, business colleagues, and so on, in each section remember to add up all your numbers to arrive at a final digit between 1 and 9. Simply follow the example below to help you work out your numbers easily.

CHART COMPARISON

John Michael Brown, born on 31 August 1962 (31.8.62) and his wife Clare Angela Brown, born on 17 November 1967 (17.11.67).

John's Personality Number is (31 =) 4
Clare's Personality Number is (17 =) 8
Their comparison Personality Number = 4 + 8 = 12 = 3

John's Life Purpose Number is (57 = 12 =) 3
Clare's Life Purpose Number is (51 =) 6
Their comparison Life Purpose Number = 3 + 6 = 9

John's Karma Number is (79 = 16 =) 7

Clare's Karma Number is (70 =) 7
Their comparison Karma Number is $7 + 7 = 14 = 5$

John's Goal Number is (20 =) 2
Clare's Goal Number is (21 =) 3
Their comparison Goal Number $= 2 + 3 = 5$

John's Personal Year Number in February 1999 is 4
Clare's Personal Year Number in February 1999 is 8
Their comparison Personal Year Number $= 4 + 8 = 12 = 3$

Now look up their final comparison numbers within the sections 1 to 9 in Chapter 7 on pages 158–207 under the correct heading: Personality Comparison, Life Purpose Comparison, Karmic Comparison, Goal Comparison and Personal Year Comparison. When you have done this then try to get an overall picture of their whole relationship together by piecing together all the different elements and by allowing yourself to trust in whatever your own inner wisdom reveals about it to you. Numerology brings awareness, and by being aware of all the numbers influencing your relationships it can help you to fulfill your potential together in life.

7

Comparing Your Charts

PERSONALITY COMPARISON 1

DIRECTION is called for in this relationship and whether this is with your family, friends or lover, you need to be sure you have the same focus or direction in mind. For example, with your partner the focus may be on family together, at work it may be a joint project you are focusing on together, and so on. At times when you lose your focus repressed feelings can build up into explosions of anger and leave you both even more directionless. There is a pioneering aspect to this relationship so you may do great things together. You may be in this relationship to help each other break down some of your major psychological patterns of behaviour, and break through to form a completely different kind of relationship together. Therefore on a daily basis it may seem like a destructive relationship you have together, for example if you are always irritated with each other, or arguing together. Destruction, however, makes room for new things to grow.

With a 1 comparison number you may be a dynamic duo and energize those around you with your get up and go, and you may draw many people to you. You can also withdraw from the world at times, and cling onto each other as you seek intimacy together. Intimacy may be an issue in this relationship, and it may be that one person in this relationship wants to get close and the other chooses to withdraw. You may prefer to remain aloof with each other, but by learning to open up to the other person it can teach you to feel safe to attach yourself and to get fully involved in order for you to grow. Life is challenging, but going for what you want together in this relationship may take you further than you could possibly think.

PERSONALITY COMPARISON 2

Your emotional connection is the most important aspect of your relationship together. That is relating to each other and expressing how you feel together as you get on with your daily lives. Support may be an issue here, with one seemingly supporting the other, while the other is dependent, or vice versa. You may also feel a lack of support or feel that you are in relationship to give equal support to each other too. You can also be overemotional and expect the other person to pick up the pieces and be there simply to help you get through the day. This number highlights and challenges your abilities to give and receive and to learn to co-operate with each other day to day. Sometimes you can be very intolerant towards each other's needs.

With the 2 as your Comparison Number then love and affection is an important aspect in your relationship. Perhaps you are very loving and caring towards each other, or perhaps you are teaching the other person to care for you because they have been closed off to love for a long time, or vice versa. The 2 influences your relationship by bringing in the nurturing and mothering aspects, therefore it may indicate a joining together to have or to look after children together. With this relationship doing things together can be important to you both. The 2 can bring warmth into any relationship, but if you are both cut off from your feelings then you may struggle to get on with your daily lives together at times. This Comparison Number 2 is a wonderful vibration for lovers because the 2 influences true romance and your daily life may well be full of roses.

PERSONALITY COMPARISON 3

There is a need for freedom within this relationship, and you may find that issues arise from demands placed upon each other's time. Sometimes conflicts may arise because you both want to do different things at different times. Perhaps you are both richly active within your lives, and separately and together you may love to play sport, socialize, work, and have lots of fun along the way. However, sometimes you can be very laid-back about life and you are learning how to relax and to simply be together, instead of always doing things together. This relationship can help you develop your sense of humour and you may be able to uplift each other when the going gets tough. Indeed, you may seem comical together in some way – perhaps the way you compliment each other physically, or perhaps you entertain people together with your own brand of humour.

Perhaps this relationship remains at a light and super-ficial level, and the number 3 as your Comparison Number can be good for casual affairs or for having lots of acquaintances, but be aware that unexpected pregnancies can happen when you are too carefree and careless. Number 3 highlights family issues. Perhaps you would like to go in deeper but the other person seems to want to 'keep it sweet', or you may want this too. For lovers and partners this number 3 can bring a terrific amount of sexual activity between you. In a work relationship the number 3 highlights your ability to be abundantly creative together. But you may have a tendency to scatter when you work together so keeping a definite focus on your goal or project may be essential to its success. With a 3 as your Comparison Number, whatever the relationship, you may overdo things together at times.

PERSONALITY COMPARISON 4

This relationship can help you both to keep your feet on the ground, as the 4 is an earthy energy, unless of course you are both highly impractical people in which case you may find your journey through life together bumpy some-times. On a day-to-day basis the 4 highlights your need to work hard at the building and maintenance of your relationship together, and to keep plodding along even when life's challenges make you simply want to walk the other way. There may well be a lot of resistance to being in relationship with each other but the 4 energy influences determination and endurance to carry your relationship through and keep going, no matter what. This number brings discipline and structure into both your lives, which can help you if you are usually scatty. If the 4 isn't in either of your charts already then it can also really help to materialize the relationship into physical reality.

With a 4 as your Comparison Number you may like to introduce some kind of routine in your relationship to enable you both to feel secure. For example, if you are dating a lover perhaps you like to go to the movies every Saturday, go rambling together every Sunday, eat out every Wednesday, and so on . . . Sometimes with too much discipline and routine the relationship can get stale, so adding some passion and romance to the relationship if it is with a lover, or changing your social routine with a friend, may be essential. With the 4, it can make issues in your relationship seem deadly serious because you can get too bogged down in the nitty-gritty. With a 4 you can bring in commitment to the relationship.

PERSONALITY COMPARISON 5

With 5 as your Comparison Number then whether you are comparing yourself with friends, lovers, work colleagues or family, be prepared for surprises because this relationship allows no space for dullness, in any form. The number 5 is a fast-moving energy and it will take your relationships forward whether you like it or not, and give you unexpected jolts, just when you thought everything was simply perfect. This can add a spark to your love life, and inject excitement into any relationship because you don't quite know what is going to happen next. This relationship may even be volatile and can leave you holding onto your hat as you try to keep up with its twists and turns at every moment. When things go too fast in your relationship you may back off, run away, or simply procrastinate. For example, when this comparison number 5 is influencing your relationship with a new lover it can mean he or she (or you) may even want to move in together after the first date! If you get a buzz from life in the fast lane then this kind of relationship may be ideal for you both.

Sometimes a 5 influencing your relationship together means that you may have issues around getting together at all, because if you are busy travelling around the world and your partner, lover or friend is busy getting on with his or her life then finding a meeting spot may be a challenge for you both. Perhaps you have fast encounters and rushed meetings, with lots of surprises too, like turning up on each other's doorstep out of the blue. Spontaneity in this relationship can be important because boredom can lead to restlessness and may cause you both to argue, or to go off in separate directions. You are also learning to express yourselves together, which can help you both.

PERSONALITY COMPARISON 6

With a 6 influencing your day-to-day life together then you know that Cupid – the god of love – is calling for you to open your hearts to each other. You may like to surround yourselves with loving and caring people, and to share this good life with everyone you meet. The 6 can also bring in heartbreak as you can both be idealistic, and if you are trying to live up to an ideal in a relationship, then glamour is ultimately shattered at some point. The number 6 also influences commitment and therefore, with a partner or lover, marriage and children are potential possibilities and potential issues too. For example, who will look after the children, and who will provide the meals, and so on. You may sometimes find with the 6 in a relationship that you are both working strongly with your feminine energies, and you may be learning to develop your instincts and your psychic abilities together.

In this relationship you can be ruled by your heart, and you can sometimes find yourself deeply embroiled in situations which you don't know how to disentangle yourself from. For example, if your comparison is with your sister who is going through a divorce you may find that you have got too involved in her affairs. You can both get obsessed with each other's lives until no one else exists. However, the 6 brings in wholeness, and by looking at different aspects of yourselves in relationship it can help you both find your centre eventually. With this warm energy in your lives you don't like to rush, but to enjoy and savour it, and you may find that this relationship meanders on and on . . .

PERSONALITY COMPARISON 7

You are trying to break through your own illusions about this relationship and the expectations about how it should be by facing the facts of what is actually in front of your very eyes, not what is floating around in your imagination. For example, with a friend who is insensitive during your time of need you may change your mind about being in relationship with him or her. A 7 can influence your relationship by helping you both to materialize it so that you are both living in the real world. It can also mean that the relationship is fragile at times because there is too much sensitivity between you both, or that one of you feels fragile emotionally. This 7 energy can also mean that you or the other feels totally open, bare, vulnerable, and unless you are willing to feel exposed then this relationship may feel too much for you. Perhaps you feel the need to protect yourselves or to protect each other too.

However, the 7 can certainly open your awareness and sensitivity to each other's needs and teach you to respect each other's openness within the relationship. You may both feel like you need space to grow and space to 'be' as well as spending time in each other's company. On a daily basis this can reward you both with personal growth by being introspective about your relationship, and learning about yourselves. The 7 brings in a very strong spiritual energy therefore you may feel a deep spiritual connection together in this relationship. Perhaps you are both interested in philosophy and religion or perhaps you take time to meditate together. However, it is possible you are both unaware of any spiritual connection as you can be very materialistic too!

PERSONALITY COMPARISON 8

In your relationship you can empower each other to be responsible and encourage each other to learn to stand on your own two feet. Perhaps you also prop each other up sometimes, particularly financially or materially. Money may be a talking point in this relationship, perhaps because you've both got it and you spend it abundantly on your-selves, or because you may argue about who pays for what, and when, and so on . . . Indeed, if you both work together in business, talking about money is essential. But if this number is for you and your lover then this material preoccupation may mean you may be talking about money way into the night, rather than having fun. Life can get very serious indeed. However, this 8 energy can also influence you by encouraging you to find other values in life, and to connect with each other spiritually.

The 8 can bring strength into your relationship, and help you both to be strong enough to face situations together in life when it is called upon, and to be strong for each other. Sometimes you may both be strong and assertive at the same time. There may also be clashes of ego from time to time, with each of you wanting to be the boss, to take control, or even to dominate the situations you find yourselves in together. You may both be bullish and stubborn and fight over the smallest of issues – like which side of the toast to butter or which seat to sit on at work. The 8 brings in strong masculine energy, and you may be interested in developing your intellect together, or brushing up each other's ego with your charisma, charm and sexual magnetism too. However there may not be space for two 'stars' in this relationship.

PERSONALITY COMPARISON 9

In this relationship you are both working towards understanding how to please each other by learning to let go of selfishness and to give instead. You like learning and you store up all the knowledge you have gained from your relationship in your head, so that you can call upon it when you are with other people in your life. With a 9 you are both strong teachers for one another, but you can also preach to each other about how things should be done too. You may kick up your feet in rebellion (if someone tells you what to do you usually do the opposite!), and let them know you disapprove. One of the reasons why you are in relationship is to learn to accept and to love each other just the way you are; your expectations can be high. You may be critical of each other too by judging each other's behaviour and on a day-to-day basis this can make for flare-ups of temper flying all over the place. Whatever you do may seem 'right or wrong' and compromise may be called for in this relationship.

With a lover, this brings in intense heat and passion and this 9 can teach both of you to liberate yourselves sexually. Your passion can spill over into your creativity and you may love to paint or play musical instruments together or to study some passionate subject together. Religion or politics may play an important role in this relationship and you may both have your own strong beliefs about life. However, you are adaptable to change and if, for example, your lover is Jewish and you are Buddhist then there is a chance you can work this out together. Equality may be highlighted in this relationship, and learning to be fair towards each other may help you both get through each day together.

LIFE PATH 1 COMPARISON

With a 1 as your Comparison Number then it may seem that you are being guided forward together and that no matter which way you try to steer the relationship it may seem to have a will or a life of its own. Of course, you both have the will to choose whether to stay in the relationship or not. It may at times seem like a battle of wills between you both, but in the end you may choose to compromise in order for your relationship to move forward in the best possible way. Indeed, you may both feel like the relationship is leading you, rather than you leading it, with the two of you simply following its lead. However, it may also be that you both accept your individual leadership within the relationship and at different times. Therefore, in that way, you do have the ability to lead or 'steer the ship'.

Sometimes, when you are both leading you may appear to be a very powerful pair indeed, but there can also be clashes of leadership between you from time to time. However, if you have a leaning towards dependency then the 1 can influence you to be independent and to rely on yourself. For example, in a work relationship you both get on with your own jobs without depending on each other. If you are both already independent people this can strengthen your relationship when you are together. Being independent can show others around you how they can get on with their lives by living and working with people and by still being able to function independently in their relationships too. At the end of the day, you can both learn from and enjoy the relationship you have together no matter who is dependent or independent, or who is leading who.

LIFE PATH 2 COMPARISON

Influenced by the 2 in this relationship you are both learning to find a balance with your lives, and somehow you may both help to balance each other out. You both bring different qualities into this relationship, and by helping to balance each other it can influence all other areas of your lives in a positive way too. People are mirrors and once you have learned about specific qualities you need from each other to help in the balancing process, you can learn to give them to yourselves too. Perhaps you are quite balanced people already, and therefore you can sometimes have a balancing effect on people you both meet together.

Part of your attraction to each other may be the inner peace and calm you both emit. However, you may equally attract disruption into your lives in order to 'test the waters' and sound out test this inner peace. With a 2 influencing this relationship a lack of peace in your home or work environment may challenge you both enormously, for example, if you have a new next-door neighbour who is very noisy. Finding your inner peace can help the other remain calm in these situations, and indeed this peace can radiate out to your new neighbours too. However, it can be helpful to note that external disharmony can be caused by inner disharmony within yourselves. And if you are attracting situations to you which are disruptive then going inside yourselves, or discussing any problems within your relationship together, may help to calm down your external environment at times. Life is a balancing act, and this relationship can teach you both about this process.

LIFE PATH 3 COMPARISON

The 3 in your relationship brings in a quality of 'beingness' which is teaching you both to learn to 'be' with each other, and to 'be' by yourself within the relationship. Learning to 'be' within this relationship may require you to be still, and to allow the relationship to 'be' the way it is, by not trying to change it, because you know that the relationship is just the way it is meant to 'be,' from one moment to the next. Being with each other requires a lot of giving too, which you may find challenging, because you are both accepting the relationship the way it is. Perhaps one person is good at being and the other is good at doing, and learning to 'be' with these opposite qualities may also challenge you both. Beingness can mean you feel like nothing is happening in the relationship, but more changes can occur from being, than from doing, because beingness means there is room for things to flow. By being together you can show others that they can be with themselves too. Beingness can be bliss because you are simply enjoying living in the moment being together.

The 3 also highlights the social elements of your relationship and when you are socializing together people may notice how much you enjoy each other's company by simply 'being' together, and how much time you spend together too. Perhaps you spend a great deal of time socializing, but this may also be an issue in your relationship, for example, if one person spends more time out socializing with people than the other or vice versa. Perhaps you have lots of different people you both socialize with together, with diverse interests and in different fields, and they may love to socialize with you both together too.

LIFE PATH 4 COMPARISON

With the influence of the 4 there may be issues around self-responsibility within this relationship, but this 4 energy can also encourage you to be responsible towards each other too. For example, with your child, perhaps you always expect him or her to make their bed and make yours too. Of course, chores need to be done, but you need to take responsibility for making your own bed and lying in it. Perhaps your child is challenged enough by needing to look after his or her own chores without others' responsibilities too. With the 4 one of you may enjoy responsibility and try to take on responsibility for the other, which from time to time may be helpful. For example, in a work relationship, when one of you is off sick, taking responsibility to get urgent work done for your workmate (of course, after you've taken responsibility for doing your own) may be necessary. However, continually taking responsibility for someone else in every way prevents them from learning to take responsibility for themselves, which is also a part of their growth.

Self-responsibility, in a relationship with a lover, may mean that you don't expect your lover to satisfy you sexually, but it is your responsibility to play your part in being

171

receptive to satisfaction and making the effort too. Once you are aware that you are contributing towards creating the relationship you are in together, you can take actions to change aspects within yourselves and to improve the relationship if you want to. This caring, responsible attitude towards each other can rub off on others around you in a positive way too.

LIFE PATH 5 COMPARISON

This relationship is testing your abilities to communicate with each other. Perhaps you are both able to communicate with each other easily and clearly some of the time and with some issues. But you may still find it challenging to talk about other issues together. Sometimes you are unable to communicate because you are not clear about what you are trying to say to each other, or because you feel if you communicate you may hurt the other person, or change the relationship in some way. Communication takes place on many different levels, and you can communicate in many ways, for example, through eye-to-eye contact, physical contact, body language, which is a major form of communication, telepathy, or communication by sending letters, faxes and e-mails, and so on. Even the colours and the clothes you wear are communicating strong messages to those around you. For example, with a lover you may change from a tracksuit to a slinky black number or a smart suit to communicate clear signals about what kind of mood you are in and what your intentions are too.

When you are confused you can give off the wrong signals, and one or the other of you may even get or give mixed signals or messages of communication. At these times you may both be unsure about how to communicate or where you stand within this relationship.

With the 5 influencing you both, being open and communicative with each other can mean that others feel free to communicate with you both. They may even be encouraged by your communication skills, and it can encourage them to communicate within their relationships. Communication helps to make the world go around, so in this relationship be aware of how you are both contributing towards the world.

LIFE PATH 6 COMPARISON

With a 6 influencing this relationship then your abilities to serve each other are highlighted. Being of service doesn't mean necessarily doing anything special, but simply by being in this relationship together you are serving each other in some way. You can also be of service by not seeing each other for a while. For example, when you go on holiday for a month then your absence may be of service to you. Perhaps you need a break from one another and that is how it is serving you both. With this 6, you may be learning to do what is best for you both, and for the group of people who surround you, like other friends, lovers, family or workmates, instead of simply thinking of your own needs, which you may be inclined to do.

Learning to think of each other can help you grow, and can help you forget yourselves. However, one of you may give too much and lose yourself by always serving the other person first. Service can mean sacrifice at times, which can teach you something about life, but you may get resentful towards each other if this happens too often.

Sometimes you may find serving in this relationship very painful, but by seeing the overall results which can benefit you both you may be willing to cast aside your personal sensitivities in order for the relationship to grow. When you serve each other and are happy to get on with it then others may be impressed, and it can teach them to serve their friends, lovers, family, colleagues and their community like you sometimes do. Just when you think people aren't serving you, be aware, they may be doing so much more than you can tell.

LIFE PATH 7 COMPARISON

The influence of the 7 in this relationship means that it is calling you both to introspect about your lives together. Introspection – going inside yourself – can help you deal with the relationship and help you to find out your own truth about what it is teaching you. Sometimes, one of you may be too introspective, and may spend more time analyzing the relationship and working things out in the head than physically seeing the other one. At other times one of you may ignore going inside to your inner self to avoid facing truths about the relationship, and about yourself. If one of you is too introspective and the other is quite the opposite it can show you both how to find a balance by being centred about this too.

With the 7 you are also influenced by intuition within your relationship. For example, perhaps you both intuitively know when the other needs time for introspection and you give each other space to do so. You may both use your intuition to help each other with your lives, like during challenging times with a little guidance. At times you may also find that if you ignore your intuition your relationship doesn't flow in the way it may have done if you had both trusted your own truth and intuition. Perhaps you ignore your lover's intuition when he or she says, 'Let's not go to that movie tonight, it will be fully booked,' and it is. Together you can use your intuition to help people around you too. This can bring to their awareness the gift of intuition, and may encourage them to be a little introspective about their lives. Together you are able to demonstrate to those around you how they can find their inner truths within themselves and therefore within their relationships too.

LIFE PATH 8 COMPARISON

With an 8 influencing this relationship then karma – or the law that what you give out you get back – plays a large part in your interactions together. Perhaps you are in a karmic relationship together because you are still working out issues together from the past. However, you also create your own individual karma as you go along, and joint karma together in the relationship too. For example, if in your life you are very selfish towards your brothers and sisters, then it may be that your partner or lover is very selfish so that you learn what it is like to have to give too. As a couple if you are both very conceited then others may treat you superficially or fail to respond to you in the way you'd prefer. Karma can also be positive and if you do something really wonderful for someone in your life perhaps in this relationship you will get your 'just deserts' and it will reward you. Of course, it is not necessary to do things in this relationship just to get a certain something back (if you do things with this intention then you may be surprised at the results) – it gives you both what you need.

With an 8, karma is helpful because it can teach you to take responsibility for what you create and teach you to be aware of your actions and your intentions too. This can in turn teach others around you to be aware of the karma they are creating, and show how that karma affects the whole world in which you live. Make friends with karma, and learn to accept the rewards and the retribution of being in the relationship you have created. These lessons can help you both to move on with your lives.

LIFE PATH 9 COMPARISON

With a 9 you are both learning about selflessness and one of the ways to learn about this quality is by being in relationship with each other. It can challenge you to give, and give, and give, and to utter no words of disagreement when you do. Of course, if you do not have the tendency towards saintliness (as most people don't) then you will understand that giving can be very challenging but very rewarding and pleasurable at times too. You may like to see each other happy and with your needs fulfilled. Selflessness means learning to give, and to make sure that the other person's needs in this relationship are met, not just your own. Selflessness and service go hand in hand, but with the 9 thinking of others first can become a way of life for both of you.

With a 9 this relationship can teach you both to work towards helping others around you in a selfless way, and they may be inspired to apply this quality in their own lives. The 9 can also influence you both by bringing in spiritual elements to your relationship. Perhaps you may both feel spiritually connected to humanity, or are inspired to selflessly serve humanity. Of course, you may sometimes need to be humble about your expectations of each other which may be high – you can only give as much as you humanly can. At these times selfishness may step in, and in a big way, and you may find that this causes an imbalance in the relationship. If one of you has been giving or given too much, this can provide a bit of a rest and help to balance things out for a while. With the 9 you may both think that humans have an enormous capacity for giving and by demonstrating this to people around you, it can spread this joy of selflessness and harmlessness out across the world, via those people around you that you meet.

KARMA NUMBER 1

In the past (or past lives) you may have been involved in breaking down each other's perceptions about life, and today you may still be breaking down those perceptions, or working towards rebuilding a new kind of relationship together. You may have in the past also been working on issues of finding your purpose together, and are continuing with this today. Perhaps you feel uncertain as to your joint purpose together within this relationship, which may also mean that you feel uncertain about the roles you play individually together too. Everyone has their own purpose in life, but there is also a joint purpose of being together within any relationship. Sometimes your purpose together can change. For example, your purpose may have been to work together, and now it may be to have children together, and so on. Knowing what your purpose together is, and redefining it when necessary, can help you work towards it.

With a 1 in the past there may have been a tremendous amount of creativity and energy being focused on moving forward together in your relationship; perhaps you achieved a lot together. Today, you may both be helping each other to develop and bring out your creative talents and to work, live or play together creatively too. Perhaps you are both creative in different ways and can teach each other about your gifts. However, if either of you repress your creative energies for a long time it may throw up outbursts of emotion, and at times hold you back from achieving your purpose together. 'Energy follows thought' and when you both utilize the creative energies available within this relationship you may both feel a strong sense of achievement and purpose.

KARMA NUMBER 2

With the influence of the Karma Number 2, in the past (or past lives) you may have both been together to develop your wisdom. Wisdom is gained by experiencing life first hand, and in the past you may have been through so many different types of situations or relationships together that you have wised up to life. Wisdom and compassion usually go hand in hand, because if you see the wisdom in a situation you cannot be angry or sad, but you have an open heart full of love and acceptance. Today you are both learning to use your wisdom together to help each other with your lives. However, with a friendship, if you do not see the wisdom in your friend's behaviour then you may react in a challenging way. And if your actions do not bring the desired results then you may eventually be wise to this reaction in the future.

With the influence of the 2 it can heighten sensitivity within this relationship, and you may drink in each other's feelings, which may be wonderful or challenging at times. Being open and receptive to each other can also be won-derful for your growth, particularly if this person is your soulmate. Close relationships with soulmates, whether they are friends, lovers or family, can make all your other relationships pale into insignificance as you are likely to focus much more of your energy on them. However, from your past together your karmic bonds or connections can feel so strong that you may feel manipulated by this relationship because it is so powerful today. However, you can both choose whether to live, work or play together and when.

KARMA NUMBER 3

In the past (lives) you may have both been involved in mysticism together in some form. For example, perhaps you were Buddhist monks at the same monastery, or worked as healers together, and so on. Therefore today you may instinctively feel a strong psychic connection to each other and you may feel drawn towards using your mystical gifts with each other too. Perhaps you simply discuss mystical subjects together, or you may work together professionally using these gifts to help others who are drawn to you. If this relationship is with a lover or partner then you may perform rituals, like using oils or herbs on each other to improve your sex life together; your instincts let you know what to do. When you first met this person your instincts may have told you that your connections with them in the past were not comfortable ones and you may have tried to give them the slip. However, in this relationship, whether it lasts for a day or a lifetime, you can learn things which may help you both to let go of the past, and to move on.

With a 3 influencing you both in this relationship you may feel like family to each other even when you aren't related. This is from your past connections together where you have built up strong karmic ties. Today, this may bring up issues for you both about being in a family. Perhaps you are critical of each other, or squabble with each other over petty things, or feel like you both need your freedom from each other because of these strong ties. You may also feel so at ease in each other's company that you spread this joy everywhere you go together. The 3 also highlights the need for self-expression within this relationship, and you can help each other develop this gift too.

KARMA NUMBER 4

With a 4, in your past (lives) together you may have been involved in building things together – a home, a family, a business or even an empire. Perhaps you were also working to maintain law and order within your lives or together for the benefit of others too. When you build things and bring in new order, it can be very exhausting, and perhaps today you are working together to finish the building process which you started in the past. For example, in a relationship with your wife or husband, perhaps you are both building a solid home for you both which will last, so that you feel comfortable to face the future together. This can be challenging for you both, particularly if you keep getting stuck at different stages in the building process. Perhaps you are tempted to walk away because this relationship seems too hard to bear at times. However it is this very building process which is important, and after every stage your feet get a little firmer on the ground, which can help to solidify your relationship together too.

In the past you may have both struggled together for your survival; perhaps you had little food, clothes or shelter to help you survive. You may have even worked together and earned very little, or been unable to find much work at all. Today you may still be struggling, even if you do have plenty of material possessions between you both, or earn an honest day's wage, because you remember the past. However, if you do have issues around your material survival in this relationship then taking responsibility for yourselves may help to improve the situation.

KARMA NUMBER 5

With a 5 influencing this relationship then in your past (lives) together you may have both been addicted to each other or addicted to your way of life together. For example, perhaps you were addicted to being rich, addicted to fun, addicted to sex or alcohol, or addicted to thinking too much about your relationship together, and so on. Therefore today you may be working together to heal these patterns of addiction together. However, it's possible you may both be free of these addictions but attract people with them into your lives, so you can help them from the inner knowledge you have learned together in the past. Today you are also learning to keep a positive mind and a positive outlook within your relationship together, and when one of you feels down, the other can add a spark of positivity to help the other see the sunshine again.

In the past you may have both worked hard to look at your relationship and life in a logical way. For example, why did your lover run away from you when you had just given birth to a lovely baby boy, even when he had good health, a job, money and a good home to go to? It seems illogical. Today, dealing with the facts within this relationship may help you both to lead a life filled with clarity.

182

Working with the reality of the situation you find your-selves in together, and being logical about your relationship can help you live, work and play together more harmoniously. With a 5, you may both be skilled in logic and be very factual people, and you can use these gifts to help other people when they find themselves needing objective and factual observations about their lives. You may both lack common sense at times, but generally common sense rules your lives and your relation-ship together.

KARMA NUMBER 6

In your past (lives) together you may have been involved in legal situations together, or situations involving justice. For example, perhaps you both were legally locked in disputes over land, or children, and so on. Or you may both have been just and kind people and together made sure that justice was carried out within your circle of friends, family, or within you local community. Today this can mean that you may feel sensitive about justice within your relationship. For example, in a work relationship as busi-ness partners you may both work similar hours, receive similar wages, or feel that what you both contribute to your business is fair and just to you both. Of course issues may arise when one person does less and wants more rewards for their efforts within this relationship.

With a 6, as a result of your interest in justice you may be constantly weighing each other up, and assessing the situations you both find yourselves in together. Sometimes you can be quite black or white about justice, and not see all the choices involved. If you are weighing up whether your mother loves you as much as your sister then this is subjective – you can't measure love – but you may instinctively feel she does or doesn't. And you may apply justice based on your feelings which aren't always right. Life isn't black and white, and in this relationship you are both learning to find the grey area of justice together. Indeed, whatever joint choices you make together in your lives can teach you about justice because people around you will soon let you both know if you are being just or not.

KARMA NUMBER 7

With a 7, in your past (lives) together you may have been princes or princesses and lived in a world far removed from ordinary daily life, and today you may still think or act like you are royalty. This may prove a challenge to one or both of you in this relationship, particularly if you refuse to live according to your means, or think your partner should bow down to you. Indeed, in real life your prince or princess may turn into a frog and leave you feeling cheated and bereft. Perhaps you both go around with your heads in the clouds, or you may attract people to you both who treat you like you are 'special'. However, it is also likely that in the past you were a nun, priest, prophet or sage, with extraordinary powers of insight, and perhaps today you use these gifts to help each other with your lives. In the past even if neither of you possessed a special title you were probably working on developing your sensitivity together.

Today you may be continuing to develop your sensitivity towards each other by being aware of each other's needs within this relationship, and by being polite and by showing appreciation of each other. Of course you can both be hypersensitive at times, but this sensitivity is in fact a gift and you can both teach people around you to be more sensitive to others too. The 7 can influence you both by making you aware of the spiritual elements within this relationship, and perhaps you are insensitive towards the other's spiritual interest at times. Although you may both be deeply connected spiritually from the past. The 7 energy can also highlight your talents, and with its influence you may both be able to call upon many different gifts to use together in this relationship, and to help others.

KARMA NUMBER 8

This is one of the strongest karmic relationships there is, and if an 8 is influencing your past (lives) together then today you are reaping the rewards and the retribution from your actions and intentions together. And also creating your karma together for the future whether you will spend it together or apart. Even if these karmic ties are evident then unless it is your fate (some things in life are), you do have choice whether to involve yourself or continue in this relationship or not. However, this can be a very powerful relationship and one which can teach you both a lot about yourselves, about relationships and about life.

With an 8, power may also be an issue, and, for example, it may seem like the relationship has some sort of power over you both, and that it is out of your conscious control. Of course, in some ways it is because fate plays the final hand. Sometimes you may both have power struggles with each other, particularly about money, or about who's taking control, and so on. Perhaps you give your power away to each other by lacking assertion at times. However, you can also both empower one another to be who you are, and to be successful with your lives, and together you may empower other people to do the same. You may both like to be the authority in your field and if this is a work relationship then there may be clashes from time to time. However, you may also see that being in authority can be a responsibility and by taking responsibility for your own gifts, and your work colleague doing the same, that is plenty. In this relationship, respecting each other's authority can teach others to respect you too.

KARMA NUMBER 9

In your past (lives) together you may have been teachers, artists, musicians, religious leaders or politicians, or perhaps you were involved in educating people together. Perhaps one or either of you were spiritual teachers too. Today you may both work in any of these fields, such as in the education system. You may also simply enjoy studying fascinating and interesting subjects together, or perhaps you are teaching each other from your own inner wealth of knowledge about life, instead of from the books you have read. The 9 also influences you both to act with care and in a loving and compassionate way. However, in this relationship you may judge each other by how much you know and how intelligent you are, rather than how caring you are towards each other at times. However, you can also teach yourselves to enjoy brains and the beauty of love, passion and creativity within this relationship.

With a 9 you are both learning to be understanding of each other, particularly at times when you both do or say things which appear to challenge this by your behaviours. Perhaps you are often hurtful towards your partner, by being critical for example, but your partner shows great understanding because he or she knows that you are lashing out because you feel hurt yourself. Indeed, their understanding may be a great gift as it mirrors to you that these uncaring words are your pain and for you to deal with, and not to hurt them. However, there is a great deal you can both learn from each other in this relationship. Together you can teach others how to be caring and understanding towards each other, once you have both learned this lesson together.

GOAL NUMBER 1

With a 1 influencing you both then one of your goals together is to find and to follow through on your objectives within your relationship. For example, one of your joint objectives may be to keep fit, so you may go jogging, do an aerobics class, or go cycling together and so on. This can challenge you both to compete to keep fit too. Perhaps one of you is more resistant to one type of exercise than the other, and you may find that participating in exercise which you like individually can help you both to fulfil this objective. Sex may be one sport which can help you both to keep fit and which you both can enjoy doing together. Once you have achieved one objective you can both move on to the next, and you may work on many objectives together at the same time, in work, home or play together.

With the 1 another goal within your relationship is to develop your mind and your intellect together. The mind is vast, and it can be stimulated by many different things in life. Anything which makes you both think can develop your mind, so you may be developing your minds all the time together. However, you are also working towards developing your intellect, and perhaps one person is more learned in literature for example, while the other has a wealth of information about art or politics and so on. Perhaps one of you thinks that you do not stimulate the other's mind enough, and this may be a challenge for you both in this relationship. However, discussing a good book or film can be fun, exciting and stimulating to the mind, so reading and going to the movies together may contribute towards your joint happiness. Your mind can also be stimulated sexually too.

GOAL NUMBER 2

In this relationship one of your goals, with the influence of the 2, is to learn to compromise with each other. Compromise means that you learn to give and take and to find a middle point which suits both your needs. For example, perhaps your parents are divorced and your mother wants to visit you on a Sunday, but you want to spend the whole day with your partner and children. In this case you compromise by spending half a day with both, which may be the answer. This results in a win/win situation so that everyone gets their needs met in some way. You may still find challenges with your decisions and feel like you are forced to make compromises, but making decisions because you truly want to, and accepting these decisions, can help both of you. Sometimes finding the middle point is easy, and at other times you both may try to manipulate the situation to go your way. However, this is your gift, and you can together show others the art of compromise too.

With a 2, fear and love go hand in hand. Sometimes you may feel cautious of the other person within this relationship, and at other times you feel totally open and loving with each other. Another of your goals, therefore, is to find a balance with both these elements, so that your fears are kept in proportion, and your loving side doesn't suffocate you both at times. Either of these can be challenging for you both because the 2 heightens your sensitivity. However, learning to listen to each other, and also learning to hear what is actually being said, can help you to relate to each other, to help you both let go of your fears, and to let you both know how much you love each other.

GOAL NUMBER 3

If 3 is influencing you both then one of your goals is to bring joy into your lives. Joy is being happy being where you are, as who you are and together joy means inner happiness from being together too. Joy can be like a state of bliss, because no matter what is going on externally you feel good. Of course, you can't get joy from each other but you can enjoy being and doing things together. Usually when one person is feeling joy it can radiate out to the other and vice versa, and these moments, or times of joy, filter into other areas of your lives too. It is infectious and other people are able to enjoy being around you both. You cannot both be expected to be joyous every moment of your lives together, but you can teach each other to be open to joy when either of you are facing challenges in your life. However, in a relationship with a lover, if you are feeling down and they are feeling joy you may feel even more miserable at times (particularly if you have PMT), because they seem happy. Sometimes you can't win!

Another goal within this relationship is to learn to express yourselves together. For example, by communicating, by making love, by touching and hugging each other, by being creative together, and so on. If you both find it challenging to express yourselves individually then this 3 energy can help to bring you out of yourselves, and in this relationship you can be shown how. Perhaps one of you is expressive physically and the other is expressive mentally, or emotionally sensitive and expressive too. People around you both may feel more able to express themselves when they are with you two. Life is always expressing itself, and this is your gift to each other too.

GOAL NUMBER 4

Finding your own uniqueness within this relationship is one of your goals together. For example, you are both able to apply yourself to life by getting on day by day. But sometimes when you both get too bogged down in surviving then finding something special and unique about each other, or indeed about the day, can help you to enjoy life and get you through. Perhaps your partner keeps your interest by dressing in a special way (just for you!), or you book a table for two at a romantic restaurant which serves food unique to both of you. Perhaps cooking is your speciality and your uniqueness shines through, or you can both smile at the unusual weather (snow in summer – phew!). At times when you can't find anything special about each other then the relationship dies a little death. It is up to both of you to take responsibility to take practical steps to inject some energy into it if you choose.

In this relationship friendship may be one major goal for you both, whether you are lovers, family, or work colleagues, and of course you may both like to build long-term friendships too. Friendship can offer you both some type of security because sex, jobs, and situations in life

191

come and go, but solid friendships remain firmly in place. You may find that your lover or partner is your best friend, but there can be challenges if one of you does not want to form these kinds of close bonds. Of course, you may both be friends even when you think you aren't. For example, you have a big argument which may seem like the end of your world, but your deep connection draws you back together again. Together you can teach others about friendship too.

GOAL NUMBER 5

With a 5 influencing this relationship then one of your goals is to find fun and adventure together. Perhaps one of you is normally the serious type in which case this 5 energy can liven you up. Or perhaps you are both fun-loving people already as you topple over each other laughing on your journey together through life. Fun is fun, but sometimes your taste for adventure may leave the other standing. For example, with a partner adventure to them may mean shopping at a different grocery store than usual, and adventure to you may mean camping in Africa with all the wild and dangerous animals roaming around. These differences can challenge you both. However, you may be in relationship to challenge each other to be more adaptable to life and to take chances where necessary in order to bring more adventure and excitement into your lives. Then you will both feel really alive.

With a 5, another one of your goals is to allow your magnetism to shine out so that you both attract to you many different types of people and situations in order for you both to grow. However, challenges may occur: with a lover, for example, if you keep magnetizing many other potential lovers to you who all wish to take you dancing at midnight! Commitment may also be a challenge to you both, and, if you don't want to settle down with your lover in this relationship, then this effervescent magnetism may be simply what you are both needing and looking for. Knowing that you are both so magnetic may also turn you both on – aren't you the lucky ones to have found each other, or lucky to be so popular and so in demand. Magnetism means that you radiate out lots of energy, and together you can radiate even more energy, fun and laughter into the world, and to those around you.

GOAL NUMBER 6

With a 6 influencing this relationship then learning about devotion may be one of your goals. For example, you may both teach each other how to be devoted to your work (if you have a work relationship), or how to be devoted to your children (if this is for a partner), and so on. Together you may also be devoted to helping others, like working together for some charity or cause. However, your devotions can get out of hand, and if you are too devoted about your partner, for example, and he or she is not devoted to you then this can be challenging for you both. Perhaps you are fanatical about your children's gifts or talents, but they may like this, if for example, you go on and on about how good they are at football. Devotion can teach you both to open your hearts to each other, and together you can teach others around you about this quality too.

One of your joint goals in this relationship is to learn to do your duty, and while some people may see duty as a chore, you are both encouraged to find pleasure in the duties you perform for each other. A duty is a task which is expected of you as a result of commitments you have made. For example, in a work relationship, it may be your duty to chair the weekly staff meeting when one of you is not around. In a relationship with children, it may be your duty to provide love and security for them, and so on. You may find doing your duties challenging, but by looking at both of your needs in this relationship you can see the necessity for both of you to follow through on your duties. You may both be communitarians and perform duties for others too.

GOAL NUMBER 7

With a 7 as your Goal Number then working on your own personal development within this relationship is high-lighted. This means that you have chosen each other to be in relationship with because there is a lot of growth which can be achieved by you knowing each other or being together. For example, perhaps your lover is teaching you about your spirituality which is another quality of the 7, which may change your perspective on life, and so on. You draw people to you to mirror similar qualities in each other, and by rubbing up against each other you usually achieve the fastest growth. When each of you goes through stages of personal development then it develops and changes your relationship together, which in turn provides more personal development for you both too. With the influence of the 7 this can help you both to connect with your inner selves and can bring a tremendous amount of (spiritual) growth.

Another goal in this relationship is to learn to keep centred when one of you is overreacting to something one of you has said or done, because the 7 energy can make people react very strongly indeed. For example, keeping centred when your daughter is having a temper tantrum can really help you to sort out the situation practically. However, you may challenge each other with the strength of your emotions which can be destructive at times, and keeping your own mind positive and strong means you can work on your own personal development too. This relationship can help you both get real together so that you can both see through the illusion of your emotions at times. Living in the real world together may require a lot of personal development, and it may encourage others to do the same when they are around you both.

GOAL NUMBER 8

With an 8 as your Goal Number then one of your goals is to find a balance between the inner and the outer goals and achievements in your life. This means that in relationship with a business partner for example, that you may want to make pots of money together but want to find value from the way you go about this together, and in the process of working together too. Often when you are focused on your inner connection and your spiritual connection to each other, you can be even more successful with your business and within your relationship. Challenges may occur when one of you is focused purely on outer achieve-ments within the relationship, or is trying to be more successful than the other. This can detract from other issues in the relationship, or it can at times encourage the other to be more successful too.

One of your goals may be to be successful together, perhaps in the business field, or successful by being happy as lovers, and so on. Success means different things to different people, but success is always something really positive. You may be challenged by your failures in this relationship, like being unable to perform in bed. But failures can be positive because they can drive you on to even greater success. Failure encourages you to take a deeper look at life, to revaluate where you are in relationship, and then to take some steps forward towards a more positive future. Success and challenges in this relationship may relate strongly to your karma, from your past (lives) together too. Together you can show others how to make the most of the successes and failures in their lives, which are facts of life.

GOAL NUMBER 9

With a 9 one of the goals in this relationship is to learn to accept each other's beliefs, and to find common beliefs which you can share together. Your beliefs influence your life and your future, because they play a large part in your make up, therefore, your thoughts and your beliefs about yourselves strongly influence this relationship. For example, if you believe that your children should be educated in one religion and your partner believes they should be educated in another then this can cause challenges for you both. Of course you and your partner may share a wonderfully happy relationship in many respects, but when it comes to your children's education then some beliefs are so deeply engrained into you both. This relationship can encourage you to let go of outmoded beliefs, and teach you new ways of looking at your relationship together too.

With the 9, one of your goals is to feel comfortable with your individual personal power, and the power of both of you together. For example, if you are the company director of a multi-national company and your partner is a leading politician then learning to relax and to enjoy the power together is important, as is learning to handle this power wisely and for the benefit of everyone. Of course power comes from within and it is available to everyone, but being able to handle vast amounts of power and responsibility is one of your joint goals and something you are both working on. This can, of course, be a powerful relationship in another way. For example, even if neither of you have a role leading a company or a country then it can still be a powerful relationship, because of the powerful lessons you are learning from each other. Power empowers others to be powerful too.

YEAR 1

With a 1 you are both influenced to seek new opportunities within your relationship together in this current Personal Year. It may be that one of you is seeking a new direction, and in this relationship you may want the other to tell you which way to move forwards. Or you may even be happy for that person to lead you. You may even try to force the other person to go in the direction that you want, because the 1 brings out a self-centred quality within you. With a 1 you can both find new things to do together. For example, with a lover you may like to explore new ways of lovemaking, and in a work relationship you may find different ways of working together, or take a new approach on a joint goal together. Of course you may both put up a lot of resistance towards new things within your relationship, particularly if some of the changes you both intend to make are quite radical.

With a 1, one of you may also find yourself taking on a victim role as the changes occur, which can be challenging to you both. Perhaps because it may feel like the world you knew with this person is disappearing. And that elements of your relationship are breaking down, which happens before new elements can begin, in order for you both to move forwards. However, you have a choice about which new opportunities to take within this relationship. This year together is a time for new beginnings and birth –

birth of a project, birth of a child, or birth of a new outlook on life together, and so on. It can be a very dynamic and exciting time together, bringing freshness into your relationship, enabling you both to find new solutions to old problems, and can add a spark of energy to your lives.

YEAR 2

With a 2 influencing this Personal Year together then finding a balance within your relationship together is highlighted here. This can mean balancing time spent with each other against time spent elsewhere (which can help to bring balance as you both feel equal within the relationship) or trying to find emotional balance together too. For example, you may both be emotional at times, and your challenges may be to steady these emotions so that there is more harmony within the relationship. Of course working on your emotions together may mean that you learn to share your feelings with each other more and learn to relate to each other on this emotional level, particularly when one or both of you have been cut off from your feelings in the past, and this can be a good opportunity to get closer to each other. Sharing or closing off from your feelings may challenge either of you this Personal Year, but perhaps by being gentle, sensitive and caring towards each other you can help each other get through.

With a 2, decision-making is highlighted and of course decisions, however small or large, can mean things go either way this year. For example, you may ask your partner to decide whether to continue the relationship with you as his or her lover, and with the 2 you also decide what you need to do. However, even simple decisions like where to eat supper together may seem challenging at times in a 2 year. Decision-making can be simple or hard work, but being co-operative and taking both your views and feelings into consideration can be very helpful. Making joint decisions can help to bring more balance into your lives.

YEAR 3

With the influence of the 3, you may both be seeking to expand your relationship in some way together this year. For example, if you already live together then you may expand by getting married this year or by having children, and so on. It may also mean that a platonic relationship with a friend develops into a sexual one, or vice versa. The 3 energy can also bring in more creativity to this relationship, and it can also be asking you to let go and relax where there is excessive 'doing' together. You may be challenged to let go and for you both to simply allow the relationship to flow in its own way, without pushing it along. Sometimes this 3 may call for a big letting go on either or both of your parts, in order for you both to expand and grow, and challenges you both to be flexible too.

With a 3 you may both be looking for more freedom in your relationship this year. Perhaps with a partner, you both want the freedom to go off travelling the world together, or you may like more freedom with a relation-ship with a family member too. This year you may both find you are trying to go off in too many different directions at once, and this may lead to confusion for a time. Perhaps you feel confused about how this relationship is expanding, and it can throw up inner conflicts, or create more conflicts between you both at times. However, taking each day as it comes may be a way of you both getting by. The 3 energy can also inject a lightness and joy into this relationship, and life in a 3 year can be a bundle of laughs with lots of socializing and having fun. Indeed, humour may be the essential ingredient which helps you both to express yourselves together this year, and can encourage you to express yourselves socially together too.

YEAR 4

With a 4 influencing this Personal Year then you may be asked to consolidate your relationship, or to ground it in some way to make it more solid. For example, with a business partner you may pour more money into a joint venture together to make its foundations firmer, and so on. You may also be resistant to change, and try to get out of your responsibilities together by being highly irresponsible, or by taking big risks within this relationship. Of course, some risks pay off and others don't, and this 4 energy can also bring in an 'all or nothing' attitude towards this relationship. However, whatever happens, you live and grow by your experiences, and this is life. This year, particularly, life may seem like hard work, but focusing your energies on your passions may mean you have more energy to give to your relationship. For example, with a lover, this may mean you have a highly romantic and passionate year of sex together and do extra special things together.

The 4 influences changes on the physical level and you may find that the very foundations of this relationship are shaken during this year. Perhaps you move home, move offices or jobs together, or perhaps a baby comes along, and these shake-ups can change your physical lives as a couple, and influence you as individuals over the long-term. Remaining practical and keeping your feet firmly on the ground can help you both this year. Getting too serious about this relationship may also mean that you both feel bogged down with it at times, and you may then some-times find the physical changes more challenging to handle.

YEAR 5

With a 5 influencing your relationship this year then expect the unexpected – anything can happen! This is because the 5 is a fast-moving energy which influences change. Perhaps you both feel more changeable about your relationship this year, or perhaps there are general changes which improve your relationship together. You may thrive off the changes you go through this year, or maybe you find these changes difficult to handle, particularly if the changes occur suddenly. The 5 energy can also test your commit-ment to each other because 5 is a highly magnetic energy which can make you more magnetic to each other, and of course to others around you. However, the 5 may help to strengthen your commitments because you may get clarity this year about the important issues within this relationship which you both would like to commit to.

With a 5, you may feel restless or feel trapped within this relationship, and at times you may feel like running away rather than facing commitments together. You can be impulsive and unpredictable, and take actions but then quickly change your mind, which means sometimes you both feel unclear about your role in this relationship. Impulsiveness may also help to liven up the relationship with spontaneity and surprise at times when life together may seem dull. However, the 5 influences communication, and by communicating with each other about how you both feel, you may both be able to see the facts and figures of what issues you are working with together in this relationship. The 5 is calling for you to both learn to express yourselves. Dancing, communicating, being creative together in whatever way, may all help you enjoy the changes which occur to you both this year.

YEAR 6

With the influence of the 6 in this year together then you are being asked to look closely to see how deep you would both like to get into this relationship. For example, with a lover, if you have only been dating six months, then one or both of you may like to get deeper in by committing further to your relationship together. In this relationship either of you may be challenged by going deeper because then the glamour on the surface disappears, the honeymoon period ends, and your idealism can be shattered. You may end up heartbroken, or get carried away with each other, or try to live up to each other's ideals too. With a 6 you may both take your time getting to know each other, and allow yourselves to meander deeper into the relationship rather than jumping in at the deep end overnight. Sometimes you may also prefer the glamour on the surface and enjoy the beauty of the visual feast rather than actually tasting what else this relationship could offer.

This 6 energy can also teach you to find and open your hearts to each other, and with a lover or a partner also teach you to find the pleasure of roses and romance together. You may be looking at your joint responsibilities together this year, and seeking to find a way of providing for you both, or vice versa, particularly when it comes to emotional security. This 6 year is also highlighting choices available to you both within this relationship, and you may be challenged to do what's best for you both, rather than only pleasing yourself. You can also learn to develop more sensitivity towards each other this year.

YEAR 7

You may both be working to get the relationship going, to really make it happen in this 7 year together. For example, in a work relationship where you have both been busy working on other things, there is the chance that you can both bring the project to fruition this year. The 7 energy helps to aid completion in a situation and this depends very much on whether you have both worked together to make this relationship good. For example, in a relationship with a new mother-in-law, your relationship may not immediately get off the ground if this is your first contact together in this 7 Personal Year. This may be because you have not worked on the relationship together previously or built the foundations. However, the 7 can also bring instant results and you may find you and your mother-in-law hit it off in no time at all.

With the influence of the 7 you may enjoy developing

your spiritual connection to life and to each other this year, and there may also be a good deal of personal development going on in this relationship too. Situations may arise as a result of this relationship which call for a great deal of introspection and soul-searching. The 7 energy may also influence you by you becoming overanalytical and you may pull this relationship to pieces in your mind. You may experience feelings of loss about this relationship; perhaps it isn't exactly the way you both want it to be. Perhaps you try to make this relationship perfect by being inventive about it instead of accepting the reality. You are both challenged to be patient with each other this year, and to trust that being in this relationship in the way that it is, at this time, is obviously exactly where you need to be. Unless, of course, either of you choose otherwise.

YEAR 8

The number 8 highlights success, money, power and sex, and so any or all of these may be issues within your relationship this year. However, all of these issues are also open to strong karmic influences, and issues from the past which you have been working on together may return more intensely to you both this year. Some issues may also quickly re-emerge and then quickly disappear from view, as you face these karmic responsibilities head on. Relationships newly formed in this 8 Personal Year together can indicate strong karmic ties from your past (lives) and can have a strong pull on you both. This year can be a year for cutting the ties that are binding you both to old ways of living. For example, if this relationship is not serving you in some way any more, then being assertive and taking individual responsibility for yourself to do something about it may be what's needed and called for.

In an 8 year you may both be constantly re-evaluating yourselves and each other, to find ways in which you can both move forward with this relationship. Perhaps while you are re-evaluating you can assert your personal power by raising issues which have bothered you, but which you have remained passive about up until now. This may be challenging for both of you and change the dynamics of the relationship. The 8 also represents spiritual will and adding a spiritual dimension to your busy lives may inspire you both. You may find that spirituality is the missing link which plays an important role in the success of this relationship.

YEAR 9

With the 9 you may both be using your minds to discriminate about how and if you both want to be in relationship together. That is what kind of relationship you may both wish to have and take into your next 9 year cycle together. For example, with a friend, if you find out he or she has been disloyal to you on more than one occasion, and talking to them about it hasn't changed the situation, then you may prefer to spend your time with others instead of with them in the future. With a 9 you can be particularly judgemental this year, and be hypercritical about each other as you weigh up the pros and cons of your relationship together. However, the 9 energy means you may also be more open, friendly, and liberal towards each other this year. You may find yourselves opening the door more easily to other opportunities which come your way. For example, with a partner you may open your door to another affair too, and with a business partner you may set up a sideline (secretly) with another work colleague.

The 9 energy can be like a breath of fresh air which inspires you to take deeper breaths as you inhale more life into you. By finding new ways and new things to do together, it can bring fresh air, inspiration and even the passion back into this relationship. Indeed with a lover, you may both be so passionate that you spend more time in hot pursuit in bed together than getting on with other things in your daily lives. This can be an optimum year for educating each other in the sensual delights, and for keeping your sense of humour no matter what. Parties loud and wild, or intimate and intellectual, may also be on your agenda together during this 9 Personal Year.

8

The Love Guide Case Studies

HERE are some real-life case studies which highlight their comparisons. This will help you to understand how to work out your chart, and also so that you can be inspired by how numerology works! Firstly, there is a married couple, Tara and Mark, next a mother and a daughter, Kate and Marie, and thirdly, two life-long friends, Annabel and Susan.

Numerology Case Study 1: A Married Couple

TARA AND MARK

Here is a case history of a married American couple who are deeply in love and who have been since the day they met. Look at their chart to see why. They have been living together for eight years.

TARA born 3 June 1969 and MARK born 3 November 1964

	TARA	MARK
Personality Number	3	3
Life Path Number	$34 = 7$	$34 = 7$
Karma Number	$56/11 = 2$	$55/10 = 1$
Goal Number	$13 = 4$	$16 = 7$
Personal Year (in February 1999)	$36 = 9$	$41 = 5$

TARA, PERSONALITY 3

Tara is bubbly and outgoing with a great sense of humour; she loves partying and socializing and likes to dress up and to entertain people. She is laid-back and takes each day as it comes; indeed she rarely worries about anything. Tara loves life, and makes the most of every moment by being very active. She paints, travels, cooks, writes and she is incredibly creative with her hands. Tara is happy-go-lucky, and she has a positive and optimistic attitude to life. She is very non-judgemental and therefore seems to bring out the best in people. She is very popular and has a bright mind. Tara can get carried away with activities, and sometimes finds she has taken on too much at once. She is a communicator, but says, 'I'm not brilliant at expressing my emotions.' She is rather untidy at times, and as a result of her love of food, puts on weight easily (not that she worries about this, she simply does some exercise). Tara is a trainer for a large bank in Tokyo, which involves lots of communication, constant use of her writing skills, and humour in the presentation of her work.

MARK, PERSONALITY 3

Mark is very strong on communication and he can and does express himself easily and often. However, he can also be prone to exaggeration at times too. He likes being around people, and likes parties and socializing but not all the time. He, like Tara, loves change, and is adaptable to his environment. He has moved countries three times with his work, which he finds stimulating, and he loves to travel. Mark is generally a relaxed person, but he is extremely sensitive and therefore can be moody at times. He likes time to think and therefore can be inactive too. He loves good food and wines, expensive holidays (like Tara) and massage, and his gift with his hands is as a masseur. He likes lots of sex (with Tara) and is very sexual. Indeed, he is very affectionate and tactile, and has a big generous heart. Mark works as an information technology specialist at a large bank (same as Tara) in Tokyo, for which he receives an abundance of money. Here he uses his self-expression, and his love for communication and caring to help people. Mark has a degree in English and has a vast vocabulary with which to express himself; words seem to roll off his tongue and he can be eloquent.

TARA AND MARK, PERSONALITY COMPARISON NUMBER = (3 + 3) = 6

The 6 influences the love of pleasure and with it a need to satisfy their animal desires. Indeed, Tara and Mark have their own A to Z of places where they have shared their conjugal rights. From A, the mile-high club in an Aero-plane to C, on the church steps in Munich, to E, in an elevator, to Z in the reptile house at a zoo; with everything in between. Sex rates high on their agenda. They are both very sensual, and work from their instincts and they really know how to make each other feel good. Tara and Mark are both very romantic, and often say, 'I love you,' and nurture each other too. They can get carried away, and can be needy towards each other, and therefore both find it challenging to be on their own when the other is out of town or not around. Sometimes their expectations of an ideal relationship means that when one of them is not being all 'apple pie' nice, the other takes it personally. However, there is great love and devotion to each other in this relationship.

TARA, LIFE PATH 7

Tara is a materializer, and likes to get things together and make things happen; she is always organizing. She has a strong imagination but is very practical, and has a real trust in the process of life. However, she is often so active doing (from her Personality Number 3) that she spends little time introspecting or thinking, and therefore sometimes gets confused or in a muddle. Tara is nature-loving, and naturally intuitive.

MARK, LIFE PATH 7

Mark is very spiritual and needs to spend a lot of time thinking and introspecting about life, and he can be philosophical too. He has an analytical brain which likes to work things out in minute detail, but he can also be imaginative and unrealistic sometimes. He is very polite, but can be distrusting of people and impatient with life, and he gets into panics sometimes. He is very sensitive and therefore can get in (and out of) emotional lows easily. He likes honesty and regards himself as a truthful person.

TARA AND MARK, LIFE PATH COMPARISON NUMBER = (7 + 7 = 14) = 5

With the 5 influencing this relationship then communication is highlighted. Indeed, they both work in this field, but in their personal life they are both working on this issue together. The 5 influences travel, movement and adventure, and they have incorporated these elements into their lives and into their sex life together too. The 5 influences change, and both Tara and Mark are thrilled by change and need that stimulation, but it also makes them feel very restless at times. They both enjoy their freedom within this relationship.

TARA, KARMA NUMBER = 56/11 = 2

The 2 means that Tara may be searching for her soulmate and believes she has found him — Mark! She loves to love and nurture, and is a caring person. Tara is learning to relate, particularly emotionally, which she sometimes finds challenging. She is also very diplomatic, but can find decision-making challenging too, particularly with important issues. Tara is a perfectionist who sets high expectations about her own performance.

MARK, KARMA NUMBER = 55/10 = 1

Mark is learning to find his own direction in life which he sometimes finds challenging. He likes to creatively work towards his goals within his relationships, and can get frustrated when his direction in life gets compromised by external events. He revels in the intimacy and he enjoys withdrawing from the world at times too. Mark has an intellectual mind which needs stimulating with new ideas and new things.

TARA AND MARK, KARMA COMPARISON NUMBER = (2 + 1) = 3

From their past (lives) together Tara and Mark are enjoying an abundance of love, happiness and success within their relationship. They have obviously worked hard together in the past to share such a compatible and harmonious relationship together. Life seems like one permanent holiday to them, as they travel the world constantly, and live and work together in harmony too. Tara and Mark are also interested in mysticism which they may have learned about in the past. They are learning to express themselves together too.

TARA, GOAL NUMBER = 13 = 4

The 4 influences security and one of Tara's goals is to work on building her inner security for herself. She likes structure within her relationship, but another of her goals is to learn to set boundaries which she finds challenging at times. Tara is persistent, and enjoys taking responsibility for herself. She loves change, and likes to take risks in life, and she loves to feel special too.

MARK, GOAL NUMBER = 16 = 7

One of Mark's goals is to work on his personal development, and finding space to think and to be quiet is very important to him. Mark is very intuitive and he is learning to trust his intuition and therefore to trust others too. He sees through people and can really feel their feelings. With his analytical brain he is good with technical details, which is important in his job, but he can get picky about small details too.

TARA AND MARK, GOAL COMPARISON NUMBER = (4 + 7 = 11) = 2

One of Tara and Mark's goals was for them to find their soulmate which they both feel they have happily achieved. Another goal is to learn to relate to each other, and as they spend so much time living and working together then they are indeed working strongly on this. Tara and Mark are also seeking to find inner peace and harmony together by sharing their lives together. They enjoy co-operating with each other, and help to balance each other emotionally. They can both be challenged by each other's sensitivity, and take care to be gentle with each other at these times.

TARA, PERSONAL YEAR = 37/10 = 1

Tara is in a year of new beginnings and seeking new opportunities within her relationship. She may also be seeking to develop her intellect, and learning and education may be on her agenda this year too.

MARK, PERSONAL YEAR = 41 = 5

Mark is in a 5 Personal Year and this year he may be working through a lot of internal and external changes in his life. Movement, travel and communication are highlighted; he may feel challenged by his restlessness at times this year too.

TARA AND MARK, PERSONAL YEAR COMPARISON = (1 + 5) = 6

Both Tara and Mark feel that they would like to start a family together, to further their commitments to each other, and also as an expression of their love for each other too. They are both family-orientated (from the 3s and the 6 in their chart) and family life is important to them both. However, their major goal this year is for them both to look at their choices and to take actions according to what's best for them both, not simply as individuals. They are working on finding a sense of wholeness within their relationship this year.

SPECIAL DATES

It is fascinating to look up special dates or landmarks within a relationship. For example, Tara and Mark's first date was on 19 January 1990, and their Personal Year Comparison for that year together was $14 = 5$. This number 5 is also their Life Path Comparison Number which means that they were both potentially aligning with their true direction or purpose in life on that date. It is also a 5 which influences fun and adventure which is their signature tune throughout their whole relationship.

Another happy date is the date they both got married, 1 December 1994, and their Comparison Personal Year for that year is a $15 = 6$, which is the same as their Comparison Personality Numbers together too. The 6 highlights commitment, relationships and family, and is also connected to the mastery of instincts too. Number 6 is also their current (in February 1999) Personal Year Comparison number, and it is this year in which they are considering furthering their commitments by having children together.

THE OVERALL FEEL

This is an unusual chart in that the Personality Number (3) and the Life Path Numbers (34/7) for both Tara and Mark are the same. Therefore this offers them the potential to explore different qualities of the same numbers together, and this can be very challenging, but also makes them potentially extremely compatible.

On a day-to-day basis they share their lives together in a very caring and considerate way, and with a great deal of love, sex and romance, and mutual respect between them. Tara and Mark share an abundant life together; they enjoy spending their money on experiences which will enrich their lives like travelling, the theatre, dining, and educational courses too.

Overall there is a lot of trust within this relationship, but at times there is also a lot of dependency too. However, they both enjoy change and are adaptable to the changes that take place within their relationship.

KATE AND MARIE

Here is a case history of Marie and her mother Kate (who is no longer alive), showing their individual charts and their compatabilities and challenges together.

KATE born 9 October 1941 and MARIE born 3 January 1966

	KATE	MARIE
Personality Number	9	3
Life Path Number	34 = 7	26 = 8
Karma Number	17 = 8	13 = 4
Goal Number	10 = 1	10 = 1
Personal Year (when Kate died, on 13.3.1994)	41 = 5	27 = 9

KATE, PERSONALITY NUMBER 9

Kate was outgoing, fun-loving, and was very liberal in her approach to life. She prized herself on being a good citizen and a good person and liked to help people whenever she could. However, she was also selfish, self-motivated and wilful at times, and she did what she wanted to do. Kate loved music, and from her Irish childhood loved dancing. She was very spiritual although in her youth she was prudish about spirituality, and fearful of her psychic experiences, but later in life became a Reiki healer. Kate was religious too, but her Irish upbringing meant that she rebelled against being 'good' at times, and was certainly liberated sexually. She was a powerful woman who set an example to those around her. Kate was very aware of taking care of her environment; indeed she was a perfectionist by nature and liked everything in its place. She could be very judgemental with high expectations, and she was often hypercritical of herself and particularly those close to her. Kate was very bright and intellectual too.

MARIE, PERSONALITY NUMBER 3

Marie is light-hearted, full of life and very creative (a brilliant cook) and expressive. She is the first to let people know how she feels and is very sensitive to their feelings too. She loves being the centre of attention at parties, and, indeed, men queue up to give her a ride home. She is casual about life, and she has no hang-ups about her physical body; nudist colonies are her speciality. She loves telling jokes and entertaining people, and has mastered the art of superficiality, which also keeps people from getting too close. Marie loves lots of sex, but affection and love are very important to her too. She is a very active and she can't sit still and constantly fiddles with things. She has a tendency to get carried away, but does not always finish what she starts as she easily loses her concentration. Marie is bright, and is prone to inner conflicts from her (socially) demanding life. However, even when she scatters her energies between many people or projects she somehow still manages to get a lot done.

KATE AND MARIE, PERSONALITY
COMPARISON NUMBER = (9 + 3 = 12) = 3

The 3 influences family issues and both Kate and Marie worked hard to resolve the issues between themselves, as a result of their separation (her mother left during childhood) earlier on in their lives. They were working strongly on self-expression together, particularly during the last year of Kate's life when a lot of their issues with each other were resolved. Marie says, 'I think we both felt complete with each other when she died.' Marie also helped to bring out Kate's sense of humour, and they learned to laugh together too. When Kate felt pessimistic Marie helped bring some enthusiasm and optimism into their relationship, and these roles were reversed at times. Marie also gave Kate a lot of massage when she was ill, and they swopped Reiki treatments, which helped them both to feel even closer and to explore their spirituality and creativity together. They were both critical of each other's behaviour and 'mistakes', but towards the end of Kate's life they both learned to accept each other too.

KATE, LIFE PATH = 34 = 7

Kate loved caring for people and looking after their physical needs, particularly as a nurse and radiographer at a hospital where she worked for over twenty-five years. Sometimes she found connecting with people emotionally challenging. Kate enjoyed the social aspect of her job, and she also loved wild parties, fast cars, and men, and was at times driven by her desire to explore life fully. She was spontaneous and adventurous and enjoyed good conversation, which was perhaps why she was so popular.

MARIE, LIFE PATH = 26 = 8

Marie is a very strong person who has from an early age learned to stand on her own two feet. She is assertive but can also be quiet, passive and thoughtful sometimes too. Marie can be very manipulative and indirect in asserting her power from time to time. She can also be bossy, and has learned that she does not always know what is best for people. Marie is a Reiki healer and she runs a successful company with her business flair, where she helps to empower people.

KATE AND MARIE'S LIFE PATH COMPARISON NUMBER = (7 + 8 = 15) = 6

Kate and Marie had strong karmic connections from the past, and they were both teaching each other to take responsibility for themselves and to find their own inner security. Sometimes there were dramas and great outbursts of emotion when they were together because they both wanted to get their own way, and they could be very stubborn. Kate and Marie were also teaching each other about independence, and helped each other to turn inwards towards their spirituality. They both possessed a strong sense of humour and they would often giggle and laugh together joyously.

KATE, KARMA NUMBER = 17 = 8

Kate had an interest in spirituality, but towards the end of her life turned deeply inside, to introspection, and to finding her spiritual connection with herself and with others. She was wealthy and materially secure during her lifetime, and enjoyed the riches she owned. She loved sex and power, but she was also challenged by authority. During her lifetimes she formed relationships with people with whom she possessed strong karmic ties.

MARIE, KARMA NUMBER = 13 = 4

Marie's mother walked out of her life when she was very young, which forced Marie to learn to take responsibility for herself. Marie was learning about survival from her past (lives). She also lived through a number of dramas during her childhood which taught her to get on with life no matter what. Marie was challenged by others' boundaries, and has now learned to enjoy structure in her life, which helps her to feel secure.

KATE AND MARIE'S KARMA COMPARISON NUMBER = (8 + 4 = 12) = 3

From their past (lives) they enjoyed gardening, cooking, painting and being creative together. They were also challenged to work intensely on expressing their feelings together and learning to communicate with each other too. Kate taught Marie about having a good time and how to let her hair down, and about feeling free to enjoy the moment. Marie called Kate by her name and never called her 'Mum'. When she died they were the best of friends, even though much of their lives apart from each other remained a mystery.

KATE, GOAL NUMBER = 10 = 1

Kate's goal was independence – which she achieved when she left her husband and children – but she often felt alone. She was ambitious with men, but not in her work as a nurse, where she was learning about intimacy and caring. She found expressing herself directly challenging at times, and people were often unaware of what was on her mind. One of Kate's goals was to develop her mind and she did this through social contact with the stimulating people she met in her social life and at work.

MARIE, GOAL NUMBER = 10 = 1

One of Marie's goals is to learn to focus on her immediate goal at hand, and to stay focused, because she can easily be led down the garden path. Marie can sometimes be compulsive in her actions and temperament, and another one of her goals is to learn to think before she jumps in the deep end. Marie had to grow up quickly, and she was independent from an early age. She is extremely creative, and often achieves her goals in life.

KATE AND MARIE'S GOAL NUMBER COMPARISON = (1 + 1) = 2

The 2 influences the emotions and they were both learning to relate to each other, which was one of their major goals.

They were also learning to weigh each other up and not to be confrontational with each other because of their differences or clashes, but to find a way of getting on together harmoniously. Through her illness Kate learned to open up to Marie and to let her get close to her emotionally, instead of cutting off from feelings which were too hard to bear from the past. Both Kate and Marie were learning to share the nurturing, caring and loving energies together too.

KATE PERSONAL YEAR WHEN SHE DIED IN MARCH 1994 = 41 = 5

Kate was searching for freedom and fun in her life in the year that she died. She had been very restless, and had just embarked upon a new career as a Reiki healer. The 5 influences changes in general, and that is just what Kate was seeking that year.

MARIE'S PERSONAL YEAR WHEN KATE DIED 27 = 9

Kate's illness and death helped to take Marie deeply into her spiritually, although Marie had also been working in the healing profession previously. Kate was in a year of endings and new beginnings, and was learning to discriminate about what she wanted in her own life.

KATE AND MARIE'S PERSONAL YEAR COMPARISON = (5 + 9 = 14) = 5

The 5 brings movement and change, particularly when life has got stuck and there is some resistance to moving on in some way. Therefore both Kate and Marie were facing the inevitable change with Kate's long-term illness and death in that Personal Year together. They worked with the changes and became very introspective, but a lot of communication also took place. Kate and Marie were also seeking freedom from commitments during that year, and were working to free those restrictions in some way.

SPECIAL DATES

Marie was age 5 when her mother walked out of her life, and 5 is the number for freedom, and change, and it was also the same number as their Personal Year Comparison when Kate died, which was a $14 = 5$, yet another 5 which reiterated more change.

Marie didn't meet her mother until she was age $19 = 1$, and 1 influences new beginnings. Marie's Personal Year Number was a 27 or 9 (which was also her same Personal Year number as when Kate died); 9 influences endings and new beginnings. During that year 1985, her mother Kate was age $44 = 8$, influencing revaluation, and the fulfilling of karmic responsibilities. Kate and Marie's Personal Year Comparison Number when they re-met was a 15 or 6, which influences wholeness, and which brought out their need to find that missing piece of themselves.

OVERALL FEEL

On a day-to-day basis Kate was very much like Marie in that they were both outgoing, friendly and popular people, and both of them were working on their self-expression and creativity. With their Life Paths, both also found

225

themselves working in the caring profession with Reiki healing, and both were taken deeply into their spirituality.

However, one of the overall issues of this chart is that they were both being challenged to accept the changes which they had experienced together, separately and then together again, in their lives. And to allow each other to mend their broken hearts from when they lost each other in the past.

Overall this is a strongly karmic chart, and they both empowered each other to take responsibility for themselves and to work with their 'just deserts' between each other from experiences they had shared together in their past (lives). They were also both strongly learning about independence and how to survive in the world on their own.

ANNABEL AND SUSAN

Here is a case history of two friends, Annabel and Susan, who have known each other since childhood, and, as they themselves say, are more like sisters than friends.

ANNABEL born 3 April 1957 and SUSAN born 28 April 1957

	ANNABEL	SUSAN
Personality Number	3	$28/10 = 1$
Life Path Number	$29/11 = 2$	$54 = 9$
Karma Number	$16 = 7$	$24 = 6$
Goal Number	$22 = 4$	$11 = 2$
Personal Year (in February 1999)	$39/12 = 3$	$64/10 = 1$

ANNABEL, PERSONALITY NUMBER 3

Typical of this 3 energy, Annabel can't sit still for long, and she leads an action-packed life. She has a carefree attitude towards life, and she is a very laid-back and relaxed person. She is very popular with her friends as she is always such a bundle of laughs. She has a dynamic sense of humour which can be very naughty, and which can get really over the top sometimes. She can be attention-seeking and loves to gather crowds around her. However, Annabel's lightness and joy means that she has a gift to be able to uplift people, and can help them to feel good by entertaining them with the frivolities of life. Annabel is extremely outgoing, and is always off to parties or throwing parties. She seems to be forever organizing social events for everyone around her. However, she sometimes finds her life in chaos as she scatters her energies by attending too many social events. Although she can handle many different things at once, she is challenged to keep her focus in life, which she needs in her work as a social Secretary.

SUSAN, PERSONALITY NUMBER 28 = 1

Susan is very independent and is likely to take off and travel around the world at a moment's notice. She loves to dress stylishly and follows fashion trends. She likes to lead her own life, and although she looks after her daughter herself, she still manages to do a lot of things on her own. Susan is very intellectual and likes to feed this by reading fine literature and studying art. Indeed, she uses her mind in her career as a pychiatrist. Susan goes for her goals in life but finds that she doesn't always give them her all because she holds back, sometimes out of a lack of self-esteem. She can be withdrawn and tends to feel isolated easily, even when she is with those closest to her. Susan is very direct and speaks her mind, usually in a caring way. She loves sport and exercise but often finds that her compulsive behaviour drives her to continue even when she wants to stop. Susan likes to rely on herself, but sometimes feels challenged when people rely on her to perform tasks for them, even though she is capable of doing so.

ANNABEL AND SUSAN, PERSONALITY COMPARISON NUMBER = (3 + 1) = 4

Annabel and Susan are extremely close friends and they support each other through thick and thin, and practically drop everything to go and help each other in times of need. They are both teaching each other to be practical and to keep their feet on the ground, which can challenge both of them at times. They are also teaching each other to take responsibility for themselves and they are working through this process together on a day-to-day basis. Annabel and Susan feel that loyalty is the most important quality within their relationship, and that their friendship ranks very high over most other relationships in their lives. They love their companionship together, and really enjoy each other's company. Their disagreements and conflicts usually arise from trying to give too much practical advice about what is best for each other within their other relationships in life. But most of the time they share a harmonious friendship.

ANNABEL, LIFE PATH NUMBER = 29/11 = 2

Annabel is very sensitive and although she can be extremely emotional at times, she is generally placid and gets on with her life in a calm way. She is a loving and caring person, and enjoys relating to others emotion-ally. However, sometimes Annabel can be emotionally needy, and she wants to feel needed by her family and friends. She loves to give, and she does it with love. Annabel is very sensitive and can easily feel rejected, and sometimes she can be touchy, moody, and defensive.

SUSAN, LIFE PATH NUMBER = 54 = 9

Susan is very liberal in her attitude towards others and she enjoys learning from all different types of people because she is really open to life. She is humble while at the same time she is a very knowledgeable person indeed. Susan is generous and warm and selflessly helps people in a loving and caring way if she can. Susan is a perfectionist and whatever she does is open to self-criticism; life is just not good enough. Susan is very friendly and finds people appreciate her kindness.

ANNABEL AND SUSAN, LIFE PATH COMPARISON NUMBER = (2 + 9 = 11) = 2

Annabel and Susan are both representing a strong feminine energy within each other's lives. The 2 represents the mother, and they do nurture and look after one another, and with great care and consideration too. Annabel and Susan are working on relating to each other emotionally within their Life Paths together, and also learning the art of sharing (which they do). They also find that they can smother each other emotionally from time to time, or are too demanding of each other's time, in which case they sometimes feel rejected.

ANNABEL, KARMA NUMBER = 16 = 7

Annabel is good at organizing and brilliant at bringing everyone together and materializing things in her life. She can feel vulnerable and sensitive, and uses her strong intuition to help her with her life. Sometimes she can be dreamy and unrealistic, and feels betrayed easily, which may be because of karmic interactions from her past (lives). Annabel is trying to carve out her own identity in life, particularly her sexual identity.

SUSAN, KARMA NUMBER = 24 = 6

Susan is learning how to find wholeness within her life. She is also learning to provide for others, which she does for her daughter, but she finds this challenging at times. Susan loves the beautiful things in life, but she can also be very critical of people or things which don't suit her. She is sensual and loves to satisfy her sexual desires which she sees as natural.

ANNABEL AND SUSAN, KARMA COMPARISON NUMBER = (7 + 6 = 13) = 4

Annabel and Susan are working on learning how to find their own inner security, but they both offer each other some form of external security by being loyal friends. They may both feel melancholic at times, but together they are encouraging each other through dramatic or challenging periods. Indeed, Annabel and Susan may also resist changes within their relationship, like when one of them needs to intensively devote their energies elsewhere from time to time. However, they are also teaching each other to find the passion in life.

ANNABEL, GOAL NUMBER 22 = 4

One of Annabel's goals is to learn to ground her insecurities by being practical, forming solid friendships and working regularly in order to find material and financial security. She also needs to learn to feel comfortable with herself no matter what. Annabel works hard and another goal is perseverance. Susan describes her as 'a real trouper who doesn't give up easily!'

SUSAN, GOAL NUMBER 11 = 2

Susan's goal is to learn to find harmony within her life and within her relationships. Making decisions is another goal, one which she finds challenging, but she uses her intuition to help guide her. However, she can be dreamy at times. Susan oozes warmth and sincerity, and she is generally calm. She enjoys counselling which is helpful because another of her goals is to learn to listen.

ANNABEL AND SUSAN'S GOAL COMPARISON NUMBER = (4 + 2) = 6

The 6 energy is strongly associated with family and both feel they are like sisters to each other. The 6 is associated with nurturing, caring, love and warmth, and indeed they are both devoted to taking care of each other – they work together with their feminine energies. They do, at times, feel neglected easily within this friendship, but they are so close and so sensitive to each other's needs that they try to do what's best for them both.

ANNABEL, PERSONAL YEAR NUMBER
(39 = 12) = 3

Annabel loves her freedom and this may be an issue for her this year. She is in a year of expansion which, as she loves social contact, may highlight her need to get out, let her hair down, and enjoy herself. She may also feel confused about which way to expand her life this year.

SUSAN, PERSONAL YEAR NUMBER
(64 = 10) = 1

Susan is in a 1 year, and is learning more about independence, and perhaps seeking a new direction in life. She may go for new opportunities, and perhaps channel her energies into new ideas, and new friendships. Susan may have issues around her self-esteem this year too.

ANNABEL AND SUSAN, PERSONAL YEAR
COMPARISON (9 + 1 = 10) = 1

The 1 influencing Annabel and Susan's relationship means that they may be seeking to break down some of their resistances to living life this year, and helping each other to find a new direction in their lives. Perhaps their relationship deepens and becomes more intimate emotionally this year, or perhaps they experience a breaking down of their friendship in some way in order to build a new kind of relationship together. However, the 1 brings in energy and vitality, and it can add a new dimension and breathe a breath of fresh air into their relationship too.

SPECIAL DATES

Annabel and Susan first met at school when they were age 13 = 4. The 4 features strongly in their chart and they were both seeking a strong friendship in their lives, at that time. Annabel and Susan's Personal Year Comparison Number then was a 10 = 1. So they were both learning to find a new direction in their lives with a little guidance and support from each other.

Annabel and Susan grew up together and at age 20 = 2 they left their country village to share a flat together, until Susan got married. This 2 features strongly in their chart; they were learning to relate to each other, and to take care and support each other too. Their Personal Year Comparison Number when they both moved to London was 31 = 4. This is another 4 influencing them to find their roots together, and to help each other to build foundations in their lives, and build up their friendship too.

THE OVERALL FEEL

Annabel and Susan are very good friends indeed, and since their early lives together have worked hard on their friendship to make it as solid as it is today. This is influenced by the number 4 which arises often in their comparisons together. One of their major challenges is to not get too dependent on each other emotionally, and to free up their expectations that the other will take responsibility for them during times of crisis. However, they are continuing to help each other to survive, and they are anchors for each other in their lives.

Annabel and Susan are learning to love and care for each

other, and it is helping them enormously to have someone to share their feelings and their lives with, day or night. They like the presence of nurturing in their lives.

9

Ending this Journey

RELATIONSHIPS come and go, but each one is there to teach you something about yourself and about life, so that you can learn what you need to learn and then move on, having grown wiser for your experiences. Numerology is life, and by being aware of all the numbers influencing your life it brings awareness to your full potential, and therefore can help you to make the most out of your life.

Numerology is fascinating because you learn that all situations and events in your life are governed by your own rhythm of cycles and trends. The more you delve into these cycles the more major patterns of behaviour, issues with your direction in life, karmic interactions, are highlighted. For example, if you are in a Personal Year Number 8, and issues around your personal power arise, then looking back to the last time you were in an 8 cycle may help you to identify the basis of this issue. Furthermore, by looking back yet again nine years previous to that, when you were also in an 8 Personal Year cycle, then the core issue may spring to your attention, and teach you about this lesson.

As with all your relationships, the lessons you are learning from each other are very simple. For example, with Life Path Comparison 1, you may be both working on independence, with 2 you may be working on sharing together, and so on. Life is simple, but the dramas that you weave as you go about your daily lives creating and working through these situations can be intricate, and a deep mystery at times. However, Numerology can help you to identify these simple lessons to help you take some of the drama out of your everyday lives, because once you have awareness 'the game's up!' and you may no longer go on playing games with yourself, with people or with life.

Indeed, everyone on this planet is learning the same basic lessons. However, each culture places its own emphasis on what are deemed acceptable experiences and relationships within the constraints of its boundaries. For example, in some countries polygamy (being able to marry more than one wife or husband) is still in practice. These relationships are natural and normal in this culture, but they are a dying minority. Similarly, there are different variations on the types of sexual relationships people have; e.g. heterosexual, homosexual, and lesbian. And there are many different kinds of relationships: with friends, work-mates, lovers, partners, children, parents, mothers and fathers, cousins, grandparents, and the list goes on. However, with numerology you can see that everyone is learning the same basic lessons just as you breathe the same air.

NUMEROLOGY LESSON IN LIFE

Relationships teach you about yourself and the lessons you need to learn in life. This numerology book has helped to highlight these lessons and has brought to your awareness your potential, and the potential within your relationships in life. This book can also help to develop your intuitive awareness as the numbers reveal their own unique magic to you.

APPENDIX

Professional Contacts

If you would like to contact a numerology school or association to find out about professional training and workshops, or to find a professional numerologist for a chart reading, please send an stamped addressed envelope to:

AUSTRALIA

Character Analysis and Numerology
Mrs C Anschutz
23 Flinders Street
Kent Town
5067
South Australia

FRANCE

Christian Gilles School
Residence de L'Abbey Royle
17 Rue Pirel
93200 Saint Denis
Paris

NEW ZEALAND

Francie Williams
North Shore Parapsychology School
60 East Coast Bay Road
Milford

UNITED KINGDOM

Association Internationale de Numerologues (A.I.N.)
Royston Cave, Art and Book Shop
8 Melbourne Street
Royston
Hertfordshire
SG8 7BZ

Connaissance School of Numerology
Royston Cave, Art and Book Shop
8 Melbourne Street
Royston
Hertfordshire
SG8 7BZ

USA

Marina D Graham
888 Prospect Street
Suite 200
La Jolla
CA 92037

B)

FM 1/01